This book is dedicated with love to my wife Wendy, who suspended her incomprehension long enough to translate and type the text.

Operating Systems: a user-friendly guide

Alan Trevennor

Σ Sigma Technical Press

ISBN: 0 905104 66 8

Published by: Sigma Technical Press
5 Alton Road
Wilmslow
Cheshire SK9 5DY, UK.

Distributed by: John Wiley and Sons Ltd
Baffins Lane
Chichester
Sussex PO19 1UD

Printed and bound in Great Britain by
J. W. Arrowsmith Ltd., Bristol

PREFACE

I wrote this book because, three years ago when I looked for it, I could not find it.

This book is all about computer operating systems, from the non-software person's viewpoint. The really unusual thing about it, however, is that I have used the three Digital Equipment Corporation operating systems, RSTS, RSX and VMS as sources for examples. Every book I could lay my hands on three years ago used IBM or ICL or some other company's operating systems in examples. Since that point three years ago, I have conducted a lot of practical, hands-on research into these particular DEC operating systems; not at a MACRO decoding level, but by daily usage of them and by probing into the way they implement the facilities they provide. All this time I have been (and am) a working hardware engineer and an enthusiastic – through struggling – BASIC programmer.

I have often heard it said that DEC RSTS (pronounced Ristus and short for Resource Sharing Time Sharing) is the most widely installed minicomputer operating system in the world. How true this is I cannot say, but it must surely be close to it. There will, therefore, be many thousands of people using it every day in many parts of the world. In addition to those systems running RSTS, the number of machines running RSX (Resource Sharing eXecutive) is also large, especially in the scientific and educational fields. The newer VMS operating system, running on DEC's range of VAX processors, will surely overhaul RSTS in the popularity stakes at some stage.

The number of people involved with these three operating systems is therefore large. It is to these people that this book is offered as a crystallisation of the things they already know, or suspect, about operating systems.

This is what I meant when I said I could not find this book. I make no claim to being the ultimate expert on the subject, but merely pass on what I have learned as an appetite whetter for the reader to use as a springboard to more academic and detailed works, after reading what is, in effect, my written-up notes.

A. Trevennor

CONTENTS

CHAPTER 4
INTRODUCTION TO AND REASONS FOR HAVING FILE STRUCTURE

CHAPTER 5
THE ERROR OF OUR WAYS

CHAPTER 6
"ON MY LEFT, THE SOFTWARE...ON MY RIGHT, THE HARDWARE"

CHAPTER 7
THE MYSTERIOUS CASE OF THE SLOW SYSTEM

CHAPTER 8

INTRODUCTION

This text is intended as a guide to the simpler aspects of computer operating systems, and is biased towards the non-software oriented computer person. The book will give an insight into the internal workings of the operating systems – without going into the fine details or getting down to the actual program listings for any one operating system. Many examples are used to illustrate the general information presented, and the actual operating systems from which these examples are drawn are listed in the next paragraph. So why do non-software people need to know about operating systems? Anybody who uses a computer uses an operating system of some kind. As most failures on systems occur when they are running an operating system it is of great value to have a clear idea of how the operating system works. This will enable the reader to talk on a higher level to system managers, who are very often heavily software oriented. The reader will also find it easier to talk about operating systems to software people. And last but certainly not least, the subject is a very interesting one and, at this level, not too difficult to understand.

Sources For Examples

The examples throughout the text are drawn from the following operating systems, all of which are products of DEC (Digital Equipment Corporation):

1. RSTS/E = Resource Sharing Time Sharing / Extended. (Examples use version 7)
2. RSX = Resource Sharing Executive. (Examples use version 4)

3. VMS = Virtual Memory System. (Examples use version 3)

The reader should not infer, except where specific attributed examples are given, that the text describes exactly any or all of these operating systems; nor, in the case of the "average" hardware described, should it be thought to be an average solely of DEC hardware. Rather, an average of many operating systems and many manufacturers' hardware has been attempted with examples to clarify the information presented, being given from the above sources. These three operating systems were chosen because of the author's familiarity with them, and because of their very widespread use throughout the world.

Assumptions About The Reader

Obviously you should be used to using an operating system, preferably one of the three used in the examples. You should be familiar with computer hardware terminology, although a glossary is included of the general computer terms used in the text. The only other assumption made is that you have a need to learn more about operating systems.

Reading Order

It would probably be best for readers with anything less than a rudimentary knowledge of operating systems to begin at the beginning and work through. Readers who do not fall into this category can probably skip chapters one and two, and start at chapter three, as they may already be familiar with the ideas introduced in the first two chapters, and can in any case refer back to them if, in the rest of the book, they discover some concept which they do not fully understand.

CHAPTER 1
Meet the System

So now we arrive at the inevitable question, "What is an operating system?" It may be defined as a set of software routines for the management of a computer's hardware resources and the orderly and effecient storage of its user's data. But perhaps for our purposes a better definition is as follows: An operating system is something which enables us to type in, "run edit", instead of this kind of thing: "Load disk 0, cylinder 10, sector 0, for 19 blocks, and load it into memory, starting at memory address 27344, unless that would involve overwriting somebody else's data, in which case try location 454435, unless..." A frivolous example, since any operating system which could understand natural English would be very clever indeed! But the example is valid, as it indicates the amount of "behind the scenes" work which an operating system must do, in order that we can use a computer with concise, predefined commands instead of worrying about how they are implemented.

As computer users we use many operating system functions. For example, its I/O handling capabilities, its various management facilities and its statistical gathering capabilities (error counting, and so on).

Let us now do a short list of the things inside the modern operating system. If the names mean little or nothing to you, do not worry. They will all be elaborated upon in chapter two, and the relationship of each to the hardware explained.

1.1 Major Operating System Components

1) I/O Section – the actual routines which make the hardware peripherals do what is required of them.

2) File processor – the body of software which controls and vets

3

information held on the system, the format in which it is held, and the general flow of information to and from storage.

3) Memory manager – on more recent systems some of this task is delegated to hardware which is external, and thus transparent to the operating system, but traditionally the memory manager allocates parts of memory to various parts of the operating system on an as-needed basis.

4) Language support – provides support from the operating system to high level programming languages like Pascal, BASIC, FORTRAN, C, etc.

5) The job scheduler – this component varies from system to system, but basically decides which one of all the users currently connected to the system is going to have the next brief period on the processor.

6) Command interpreter – interprets commands from user.

Everybody you ask will give you a different list, but the above cover the major areas of the typical operating system.

1.2 Hardware Interface and Management

The section of the operating system which deals with hardware resource management will obviously vary greatly from machine to machine, partly because of the difference between the machines they run on, and partly because of the degree of control required. An example of the hardware interface and management section of any operating system running on DEC's 11/34 processor, such as RSX or RSTS, is the software to run the memory segmentation hardware which is used to increase the memory size above that which could normally be addressed with a 16 bit address bus. The hardware interface and management section depends upon the methods used to run the hardware. An example of this is hardware-interrupts; RSX being a non-interrupts driven system, would require less of this kind of software than RSTS, which is interrupt-driven. If the definition of the hardware management section of the operating systems is extended to include things like the hardware clock or the power fail detect mechanisms, then there is a fairly wide spectrum of operations covered by it. Broadly speaking, controllable bits of hardware which are not ruled by an I/O driver will probably fall under the control of the hardware management and interface software.

Facilities Provided

A modern multi-user operating system takes a huge amount of time, money and effort to produce. It costs more of the same to maintain, extend and update to new versions. Accordingly, at the early stages in planning a system, there must be a fairly good idea of what type of computer users are likely to buy it. There are many categories of users, all with different, often conflicting, requirements. Some of the major groups are listed below, along with the sorts of things they are likely to need from the operating system they buy.

1.3 Operating System Users – The Major Groups And Their Needs

1) Commercial users – fast access to large bodies of simple statistical and textual information, plain, easy to understand system commands and procedures and error messages, easy modification of programs written in high level languages, as little involvement as possible in machine specific details, maximum assistance to hardware maintenance engineers to obtain fast repair times, information security between users and outsiders.

2) Scientific users – easy attachment to the operating system of specialist devices, easy interchange of information between users, great mathematical precision, good handling capability of large array types of data, easy modification of the operating system code, mostly: speed of processing secondary to absolute accuracy.

3) Educational users – good small file handling (10 classes of 20 students, all with a ten-line program!), on-line help messages, error messages must be clear and concise, good support of the more popular high level languages, must be good at terminal I/O and provide fast response times under a heavy terminal load, must have good security between users to prevent student experiments or mishaps seriously jeopardising other users' data or the operating system itself.

It should be obvious from the list that no one operating system can hope to satisfy all these requirements; for example, RSTS may satisfy 1 and 3, RSX may fulfill 1 and 2, but in general no one system will be totally satisfactory for ANY application. Listed below are the kind of things which will decide the customer to whom it will be attractive.

1.4 Operating System 'Musts':

Terminal handling.

Hard copy print-out capability (i.e. must provide an ability to drive printer).

A set of error messages.

A set of predefined commands.

Some kind of documentation for use in training – the fuller the better.

A set of minimum utility support programs to implement these functions.

Most important to the vast majority of users is the ability to store and retrieve information from attached peripheral storage devices.

Market deciding factors: operating system additions.

Statistics gathering (a great help in obtaining and maintaining system efficiency – see chapter seven).

Ease of expansion of hardware (a lot of people discover to their cost that the operating system they bought a year ago is only able to run five terminals, and that they now need seven).

The degree to which the system may be tailored to specific installations requirements.

Support for very large file sizes (data base users would be attracted by this feature).

A foolproof data protection system between users, or between users and the outside world.

Command style – an operating system where the command syntax is variable may not be a good selling point to the inexperienced or infrequent user.

User friendliness – this is the industry term for the quality of the terminal user-to-operating system interface; where this is good an operating system is said to be "user friendly".

Simplicity (or otherwise) of system procedures.

Good mechanisms for passing messages between user terminals (e.g. the MAIL utility of VMS or the TALK program of RSTS).

Comprehensive logging of hardware errors – this factor decides to a large extent how long a system takes to fix for all but the most obvious faults.

A cacheing capability (see chapter six).

Portability – it is nice (though not common) to have an operating system which can be translated between different manufacturers' machines, and look reasonably similar once this is done. Operating systems like UNIX are the exception to this rule.

This list is not complete, since a whole range of decisions need to be made about the high level language support: to what degree should the language system do its own I/O, what measure of autonomy, as regards access to system facilities, shall the language systems be allowed, and so on. As I have already stated, an operating system is a very complex and expensive thing to produce, and must be aimed carefully at its market. The brief history of the computer industry is littered with the corpses of expensively produced operating systems which aimed for the mass market by pleasing everybody and ended by pleasing nobody, as in the fable. The decisions taken at the design stage are thus very important with regard to its success – along with other factors such as which machines the product is to run on, marketing and publicity efforts, after-sale support, and so forth.

CHAPTER 2
Major Operating System Components Described

2.1 The file processor.

A file processor performs a great many functions, almost all of them highly complex. Its primary purpose is to process the retrieval and the storage of information (files). And indeed this is the component which imposes and maintains the file structure. (File structures are introduced in chapter four.)

The operations of the file processor cover a wide range, but let us start with an example drawn from RSTS. Any user who types a command to run a program, or perhaps load a file from disk for listing or modification, or any other operation which requires transit of information from the file storage to the user's area of memory will have his request formatted into an entry in the file processor's request queue. After all other entries in the queue above it (or with higher priority) have been serviced, it will be serviced itself. First the file processor will decode the operation to be performed, and break its execution up into a number of steps for completing it. For our example: the loading of a file into memory. The steps would look like this:

a) Perform a verification of the file-name supplied. For various reasons most operating systems disallow certain characters in file names. As an example, try typing the command "old FIL?23" to RSTS. The result is, because the question mark character — ? — is not allowable in an RSTS file-name, the error "illegal file-name" is given in response. This occurs before the file processor even accesses the directory to see if the file exists.

b) The directory belonging to the user (or an alternative one which he may have included in his command) is located and searched for a file whose name matches the one in the command. If the file processor finds the match it is looking for, then the information about the file which is stored in the directory along with its name is passed on to the next stage. If the file does not exist in the specified or default directory the user is informed that the file processor "Can't find file or account". Note that this error also occurs as its text says if the specified account directory cannot be found.

c) Using the information about the file passed on from the previous stage the file processor now sets about converting the information into a parameter block for an I/O operation, subject to the proviso that the user has not tried to load a file which he has no access rights to, or that another user has not already got the file open for writing new information into it. If either of these conditions are met the error "Protection Violation" occurs, the file processor goes on to its next request and our user must remedy the situation, perhaps by logging into another account from which he can access the file or by waiting until the current access to the file is completed, then try again.

The format which I/O drivers require for their parameters is usually quite strict. It has to be, otherwise the I/O driver would be far bigger than it needs to be. The file processor knows this format and converts the information from the directory into a set of or maybe several sets of parameter lists to be put in the I/O driver's parameter area or queue. The descriptor information contained in the RSTS directory is listed and explained in chapter four.

d) When the file has been loaded into memory by the I/O driver the driver signals the file processor that the job is done and the file processor then ceases its involvement. The user's statistics must be updated to show what he is running. The program is now ready to run.

The same kind of sequence will be executed when a user program requests some data to work on, or requests that a file be updated are encountered – though, of course, when a file is to be updated then the directory information must also be changed.

I have grossly simplified the steps in the example above, since it makes no mention of the run time system interaction which occurs in almost every case, nor does it take account of any cacheing schemes which may be in operation. In addition, the directory file-names are stored in a format called RADIX 50 (this is a means whereby a restricted character set may be stored with three characters in a 16-bit word, thus reducing by one/third the space required to store file-names – important in some applications). Before the file-name in the command can be matched to the ones in the directory one or the other must be changed so that they are in the same format. However, even with these omissions, the description is still valid as an overview.

As already stated, the file processor is a complex block of the operating system, and a few of its other likely functions will now be considered.

System protection: the system must protect itself from access by unauthorised users and malicious interference from people who may want to steal or destroy information held on it. The system's rightful users may want to be protected from cross-accessing between each other's information – as in the case of a computer bureau – or the same group of users will require a mechanism to prevent two of them attempting to access the same file for update simultaneously. Security against the outside world is usually attained by a password arrangement, where the user has to know a system account name or number, along with its password in order to log-on to the system. Non logged-on users can usually access very little or none of the information held in the system's filestore. As an interesting sidelight on passwords, most systems do not print up the actual password as the user types it in since this, especially on a hard copy terminal, would greatly aid anybody who wanted to look over his shoulder or look at the paper log later to discover the password. VMS passwords are not displayable at any stage; no matter how priviliged the user, all the accounts on the system have a password but DEC have distributed no utility which can be used to display them, and the password is held in the system in a scrambled form for which the de-scramble algorithm is not published. Thus, when a user types his password it is scrambled and the output of the scrambler is compared to the version held in the SYSUAF.DAT file to decide if it is correct.

Log-in control: in addition to the password monitoring described above the file processor may have also to control the creation of an entry in the systems list of the jobs it has currently in hand. When a new user logs in this list (or table, as it is called in most cases) has to be modified. This is also the case when a user logs off the system.

Inter terminal communication functions: this includes things like the RSTS "broadcast to a terminal" facility used by the RSTS "UTILTY" program in the "SEND KBn message" command, or the VMS "REPLY" facility, e.g. "REPLY TTAn: message". The whole range of operations can be run by the file processor, though this is not always the case.

Some hardware control: as an example, the RSTS file processor can disable a terminal. The RSTS "UTILTY" program implements this function with its "DISABLE KBn" command.

User Priority Controls: this is a feeder function to the scheduler (see below under component "5"). Users' priority ratings are changed so that the operating system will give those with higher priority longer, or more frequent, bursts of CPU time. Almost all multi-user systems now feature user prioritising. However, the reader may know of some older operating systems where the concept is not implemented. Basically, the file processor will check the parameters specified for the change in the priority level and, so long as they are within a predetermined range and the requestor has the necessary system access privileges, the table of users which the scheduler employs is updated to show the new level of priority.

The file processor is often the operating system component via which the system statistics are obtained. These include the names of logged-on users and the information about the system resources they have consumed (e.g. C.P.U. time), or have assigned (e.g. devices). Other system statistics may be hardware error counts (as distinct from error logging) and the system date and time; also system performance statistics may possibly be supplied via the file processor. As examples of these kinds of information, the statistics displayed on a RSTS system by the "SYSTAT" program come via a SYS call to the file processor. Under RSX the "RMD" utility displays the statistics, and under VMS the "MONITOR" program performs the same function.

The file processor must include mechanisms for creating and deleting user accounts on the system. Very often a system manager chooses to segregate users of the system. The company ledger programs may be run from one account, whilst the stock control programs may be run from another. When the system manager gets a new set of programs for a third function (perhaps word processing) he will probably want to create a fresh account to store the new programs in, and, optionally, for users to log into when they want to use the new software. Bearing in mind the file processor's direct responsibility for the file structure, it is a natural choice to implement this create/delete account function. When a new account is added the file processor must add an entry into the master (or root) directory, describing the new account and giving a pointer to its sub-directory location, and perhaps some other details about it. Of course, when an account is deleted the reverse procedure must occur. See chapter four for a detailed look at directories.

The file processor must control the creation and deletion of files on the system; indeed, the usefulness of a computer in information storage hinges on its ability to access, extend, edit, create and delete information held in the system storage media. The mechanics of creating and deleting files is fairly similar to those for adding or removing accounts, except that here the directory that gets updated is not the master directory but the users' directory. Naturally, the file processor must check that the requesting user (or his program) is allowed to perform the required operation.

The file processor, then, is a very complex part of an operating system. Indeed, it is on many systems the major part of the operating system. In many cases the file processor is so complex that it can only progress one user at a time. Where this is the case a hardware problem may occasionally cause the system to hang up — that is, still appear to be running, but not respond to any commands which are typed in. Some examples of how this can happen will be examined in Chapter Five, section 4.

2.2 I/O drivers.

I/O (input/output) drivers — sometimes called device drivers or device handlers — are the part of an operating system which are directly in charge of hardware devices and, acting on instructions from other parts of the operating system, make the devices do what is required of them to implement the input or output of the required information. I/O drivers are only rarely "aware" of the type of data they are passing in or out of the computer; cases where they can be said to possess this ability are on small micro systems where the distinction between different operating system components is more blurred because there is only a single user of the system.

The range of complexity of I/O drivers is very wide, ranging from what is often considered the simpler type, like a line printer driver, to the more complex drivers: for example, a disk subsystem driver or a magnetic tape driver. The complexity of an I/O driver is dependent on the device it drives and the level of sophistication which that device operates at. I/O drivers usually receive the parameters for a single operation in a set of memory locations called a parameter block. In almost every case the parameter block will specify the following minimal information:

The operation to be performed; for drivers which control more than one of the same kind of unit, the unit number on which the operation is to be performed.

The values to be used in the device operation to make it perform the required operation.

A place to report any errors or a successful completion.

The data buffer address: i.e. the address in the memory to be used to load data to or from.

Because I/O drivers deal in the rough, tough world of human-controllable devices they should be able to deal with any known set of conditions occurring within the device which they control, including, of course, any correctable faults within that device. This is not too difficult in our simple case line printer driver, as the most in the way of status signals we would expect to get from line printer registers is two — not including interrupt-related signals. The two signals in the status register of our theoretical line printer will be called "ready" and "on-line". "Ready" signifies that the printer is ready to accept a character for printing; "on-line" shows that the printer has been switched into its on-line condition with paper installed. This is a more complex status signalling arrangement than many line printers have; a more usual set up is to have just one "ready" signal, which signifes "paper in", "on-line" and "ready to accept a character". Now if, for example, the printer runs out of paper, its internal logic will detect this and the I/O driver will see the on-line bit in the printer's status register go from true to false, so the I/O driver must obviously check that this has not occurred before sending data to it for printing or data may be lost. Given that our theoretical printer has these two status bits we can draw up a small table of all the possible combinations which may occur, and list what our line printer I/O driver will do for each combination. See Figure 2.1

Line printer status signals truth table		
'Ready'	'On Line'	Printer I/O Driver Action
False	False	If any characters to print then issue 'device offline' message
False	True	Same as for both false
True	False	Wait till printer is ready for a character (maybe with timeout)
True	True	Send the printer a character

Figure 2.1

LINE PRINTER STATUS SIGNALS TRUTH TABLE

There are some complications to this apparently simple I/O driver (you knew there would be). A line printer prints a line of characters at a time, that is, the computer sends the printer enough characters to make up a line of print (commonly 132), and then some kind of terminating character which the printer interprets as a "print now" command, and obediently prints out all the previously sent line which it has stored in its memory. The complication arises when the computer is in the middle of sending a line of characters to the printer and suddenly detects a fault. The printer has dropped off-line. Now the I/O driver must issue an error message to get the printer back on line. Once this has been done the user or his program may request that printing resume at the exact point where it was interrupted. If the I/O driver had already sent the first few characters of a line it would resume sending at the next character subsequent to them. However, the printer may have lost these already transmitted characters due to being powered off while the paper was replaced or the fault condition cleared etc., so these few characters – which might be the bottom line of your salary advice, for example! – have been lost, and the whole print may have to be done again. How much better, then, if the printer's I/O driver were to resume printing at the start of the line, if there seems suffcient reason to do so. One further point is that many I/O drivers have a time-out facility; in our line printer this could be used to good effect in the following case. The printer has just been sent a character. The printer I/O driver waits for the printer to become ready to accept the next character, but the printer cannot do so because the printer cable has been accidentally disconnected and will not be able to signal "ready" until the fault is rectified some hours hence. In the meantime, the printer's I/O driver will sit in a "wait" loop, using up processor time and giving no outward indication of what is wrong. The solution is to have the I/O driver apply to a module of the operating system for a time-out. Any I/O driver (or other system component) which is beginning an action which might conceivably lead to a lock up may request that the timer service cause an action to be aborted and an error message printed to the user — if the request is not cancelled by a successful completion before the time-out expires. This timer service module must be able to handle many requests. But if the system clock can be used the I/O driver may do its own time-outs. As a specific example, I have witnessed a faulty line printer on a RSTS system which, to all outward appearances, was ready and on-line with paper installed. Unfortunately there was a fault on the printer servo which it could not detect. This prevented its "print a line" cycle from starting. Consequently, after a time the message "device hung or write-locked" appeared on the terminal and the job aborted. This was a time-out error and it is to deal with such situations that RSTS and many other operating systems have this time-out capability.

So much then for our "simple" I/O driver. The more complex variety are used when more than one device is connected to a controller. These are usually magnetic tape, disk or terminals. Let us take as our complex example a disk controller which can control up to four drives; but let us go easy, and say that we are only going to use two of them! The three most basic operations which any disk controller must handle are as follows:

1) Move the read-write heads from their current position to a new one (seek).
2) Read a sector.
3) Write a sector.

For the sake of simplicity in this example we will assume that our disk controller does not possess the ability to perform the more complex functions like write-check, or have programmable transfer burst capability. Let us examine in a little more detail how the functions listed above may be programmed into our disk controller. A "seek", for example, is often an "initiate" function, which means that the controller need only initiate a "seek", then there need be no further controller supervision, so that a second drive can be programmed to do something else whilst the first is seeking. This makes the most efficient use of the controller. When the first drive has completed its seek operation it can raise an interrupt to signal that the drive's read-write heads are at the required position. Then the I/O driver may perform the required transfers to carry out the function demanded of it. Some operating systems give the option of using this overlaped seek capacity or not, and there are many opinions as to how much benefit they gain, but the overall idea seems a good one and should, if properly used, increase the efficiency of the disk sub-system as a whole, especially where there are a number of drives connected to a disk controller. As already stated the contoller needs to know the buffer address in memory where it is to obtain data from, or load data into. This is only applicable when the controller has direct memory access capability, since in all other controllers the data from disk must be transferred under constant supervision of the processor, a much less efficient method.

The only point about the memory buffer (sometimes called a sector or cluster buffer) address which is supplied to the controller is that if any complex memory paging or management hardware is in use the disk I/O buffer may have to be located within a part of the memory which can be accessed without using this special hardware. This, however, only applies to memory management hardware which needs special setting up, rather than to the kind which does paging on the addresses present on the computer's address bus. We must, in a multi-drive environment, tell the controller which drive the operation is to be carried out upon. Assuming that the operation is a seek we must tell the controller to what location on the disk surface we want the drive to seek. Finally, with the read or write sector functions, we have to identify which sector we want the data to be read or written to or from. An additional feature often provided is the number of bytes-to-transfer count. This is most valuable where a file is contiguous (see glossary) and the controller can set up with the sector number to begin at, and then be made to continue reading or writing to all subsequent sectors until the required number of bytes have been transferred, so that, for example, to write three sectors starting from sector one to sector three, we program the bytes count to 1536. (Equals three times 512, 512 being a common number of bytes per sector.) We program the sector required as one and then write into the controller's memory register the address of the data to be written, then put the code for a write command and the value for sector one into the controller's command register. Then the operating system can take over until the controller indicates that it is finished with an interrupt. The fact that during the transfer the computer's bus is being contended for by the disk controller, the processor and possibly many other devices is quite transparent to the operating system. Because this contention is all resolved by hardware arbitration logic as far as

This diagram shows the organisation of a disk with 8 sectors, and an unspecified number of tracks. Note that the under surface of the platter illustrated may also be used for recording, this will give double the capacity shown.

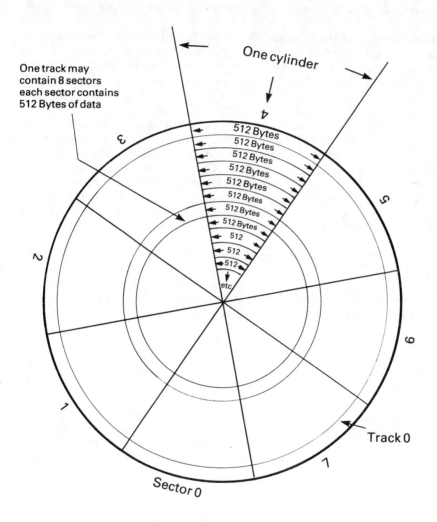

Figure 2.2: Disk Organisation

One sector contains 512 bytes (typically)
One track = a set of sectors at an equal distance from the centre of the disk.
One cylinder = a set of tracks arranged one on top of another through the entire set of recording surfaces.

Figure 2.2: Disk Organisation

17

the operating system is concerned, the I/O driver can proceed no further until the transfer is completed. It is thus more profitable for it to get on with something else for another user until the transfer is completed, then wake up the I/O driver to proceed with writing more data or preparing to handle its next transfer for some other user.

Having looked at the way an I/O driver for a disk controller sends its commands, and information to implement these commands, to the controller, let us look at the flow of status information which the controller supplies to the I/O driver software. Disk drive units and disk controllers provide varying amounts of status information from type to type. Some provide information on just about anything the software might possibly need to know. Others provide the bare minimum. In any case, the I/O driver needs to know as much as possible about what is going on in the devices which, via the controller, it is in charge of. The I/O driver must read the status information for any of the drives upon which it wishes to perform a function, both before it is performed (to ensure the unit is ready) and after it is completed (to check for a successful completion). The kind of status indicators present on many disk drives are listed below:

1) Ready – the unit is ready to perform any of the functions of which it is capable.

2) Sector count – indicates that the sector shown in the register is now under the read/write heads of the disk drive.

3) Write protected – the unit currently has its write circuits disabled, to protect the data on a disk during a copy procedure, or other times when data on a disk must be guarded against erasure.

4) Error indicators – commonly the kind of errors which may be shown here are "data error", where the data verification hardware has detected that data has been read incorrectly; "servo error", where the disk drive's error logic has detected some malfunction of the disk read/write head positioner servo; "speed incorrect", when the speed of the disk is too high, too low or unstable; "data late", when the drive cannot see any data coming from the read/write heads after a fixed time-out period has elapsed during a read function. These are the main types of error which may be signalled to the I/O driver. Many refinements, additions and alternative names for these signals are implemented on disk systems currently in use.

In most controllers the registers which are used to provide commands and information to program the controller are also readable, so that these can provide limited information about the disk unit currently selected. Given all these different commands for each of our drives, it is inevitable that the I/O driver for our disk controller will be more complex by far than the line printer example mentioned previously. Some basic considerations in writing such a device driver will now be discussed.

The comments made in the line printer I/O driver about a time-out being imposed on a peripheral operation may still apply here when the disk drive units concerned are only simple ones like many floppy disk units. However, most non-floppy disk drives (i.e. hard disk drives) and even some floppy disk drives will have, built into each disk drive unit, some degree of error detection circuitry. This will include a time-out on functions like "seek", "return to O" (sometimes called "recalibrate") or "read a sector". This works by imposing a time-out on an underway operation. If, when the time-out expires the operation is not complete, or in some of these cases, at least not underway, then the drive signals an error to the controller, which in its turn signals to the I/O software controlling it that the error has occurred. The "hard" disk unit will mostly run on controllers which possess direct memory access (DMA) capability, thus simplifying the I/O driver's involvement with data transfers considerably, and making the amount of CPU time consumed by the disk I/O driver much less than if it had to effect the transfer of every byte of data directly. Disk storage technology has advanced by leaps and bounds in the past few years, with many disk drives now being installed in office environments being able to equal or exceed the information storage capacity and performance of the now elderly, "washing machine" type of drives, so called because they were about the size and shape of a twin-tub. But however much the technology and performance of disk storage devices may improve, there are still situations which occur when the drives fail or malfunction. When this happens the disk I/O software must deal with them, and if possible correct the fault, or re-try the operation. This question of re-tries is often one which is decided at the design stage of the software, and the decision is of the utmost importance to the perceived reliability of a disk sub-system. Should the disk I/O software "hide" errors from the user by re-trying a failed transfer a number of times and not informing the user that the re-tries have occurred, or should any error encountered during a disk transfer result in the user's progress being halted with an appropriate error message? (In other words: no re-tries!) The usual solution is of course something between the two. A disk operation is re-tried N number of times, and each re-try is counted as an error. But unless all re-tries fail the user carries on with the task he is working on, and can only discover if there are re-tries happening by looking at the error log or error counts which the operating system keeps. If the errors go unnoticed for the time it takes the fault on a disk drive to get to the stage where its performance is so degraded that even re-tries cannot make it function, the system users are made suddenly aware of the problem when the unit in question becomes unusable. This leaves the somewhat crucial question of how many re-tries should be done. In their manuals, disk drives' manufacturers usually include a section on the subject of the software interface to their machines, and I have found that many manufacturers recommend that four or five re-tries be made after a failure. However, if we look at our three sample operating systems, we find that many VMS disk I/O drivers seem to go for eight re-tries, whilst RSX does sixteen and RSTS re-tries twenty-one times. These figures can be altered, but with systems as distributed are the usual number.

We could list the pros and cons of a great number of re-tries, but the list would be long, and would not really make up your mind on all applications. I think it better to say that in my opinion, on a system where it can be confidently expected that the system manager will keep a regular check on the system error log's content, a large number of re-tries may be advantageous, since the system manager can notify his hardware maintenance engineers before the fault gets so bad that there is a possiblity of a data error getting written on to the disk undetected in spite of the error-checking mechanisms. This risk must obviously increase with more re-tries on a faulty machine. If, on the other hand, the system is small, with a manager who is not full time – someone, for example, whose job is really chief accountant and who runs the computer between times – the number of re-tries is probably better set low, as if errors occur they are more likely to go unnoticed, and if a high number of re-tries were in operation a data or directory corruption could get through and be copied through all the copy disks before anyone is aware that the fault exists. Thus the closer the watch on the error log, the quicker the problem can be rectified, and so it does not matter much if many re-tries are performed, since the risk of corruptions slipping through is known to exist and can be watched for until the problem is remedied. One further point about disk re-tries is that where they are occurring in signifiant numbers they will slow down a system considerably (See Chapter six).

The next major consideration in writing a disk I/O driver touches the way in which disk transfers take place. The subject of file and directory fragmentation will be dealt with in chapter four, but let us look briefly at the concept of contiguous storage and how it can improve the efficiency of our I/O driver. Almost all "hard" disks which use a sectoring format use a block size of 512 bytes (often expressed as ½kb = ½ a kilo byte). This is illustrated in Figure 2.2. Now we have already seen the way in which some controllers allow the software to specify how many bytes of data are to be transferred and that, if more than one sector of data is specified, they will go on to the next sector following the one currently being read/written. If the controller has this capability whole tracks may be read or written at a time. If there are 32 sectors on a track, each of ½kb, the byte count register need only be set up to read/write 16kb (32 times ½kb) and the I/O driver's involvement is minimal. There are drawbacks to transferring this much data in one go, but the principle is valid, since using this method we only program the controller registers once, instead of 32 times, effecting a considerable saving on CPU time consumed by the I/O driver. Thus, while our large transfer is taking place, the operating system has the use of the CPU and can perform other useful work. This large transfer capability is only useful where contiguous storage is available, and again, that brings with it a few problems. But on balance the method is useful since it renders the I/O driver more CPU efficient and that, in the thick of a multi user operating system, is important. Chapter four deals with the concepts of disk optimisation and contiguous storage, as well as the concept of clusters (or buckets).

When two of the disk drive units attached to our theoretical controller both complete an operation simultaneously, they both raise an interrupt at once to signal the fact. The controller may give one or the other the greater priority so that, when the disk I/O driver runs in response to the interrupt, it will only see the higher priority drive as being in need of attention. The second drive will cause a further interrupt immediately after the first has been completed, and this time the controller will show the I/O driver the second drive as ready. In this scheme the I/O driver sees only one drive per interruption ready for service. In a second set-up the controller shows a bit true in its status register for every drive which has an interrupt pending. In this case the I/O driver must decide which of the interrupting drives it will attend to first. In most cases the decision is not a difficult one, since if, for example, the first drive has just completed a "seek" to a new cylinder, whilst the second one has just completed a read operation, it makes no great difference which of them is attended to first. In some cases, though, the order of response to two simultaneous interrupts may be important. Consider the following case: drive one has just ended a write operation, while drive two has been programmed to seek to a new cylinder. Drives one and two both raise their interrupt lines at the same instant. Drive one is reporting a successful read, but drive two is reporting that it has detected a servo fault in its head positioner electronics. Drive two may be subject to a failure which is making its head postioner drive flat out towards the centre of the disk – and disaster (i.e. a head crash). Obviously, drive two should be serviced first, and its heads retracted and, if possible, the drive run down so that the duration of the fault is lessened. In the real world, however, many disk I/O drivers just scan the drive status register and test for each drive in turn to be active, without going so far as to poll each drive for what it requires. This example goes to illustrate that a disk I/O driver must to some extent make intelligent decisions about what it is doing. Also, the disk I/O driver should make maximum use of the disk drive and controller's facilities to reduce the time which the I/O driver ties up the C.P.U. for.

That concludes our look at the two I/O drivers which you could find working within an average minicomputer operating system. Many points have been glossed over, since they are beyond the scope of an introductory text such as this, but in any case I hope that the discussion has stimulated an interest in this, most hardware-oriented, part of the operating system.

2.3 The Memory Manager.

Time was, and not so long ago, that a computer's memory was its weakest point. There wasn't much of it, it was slow, it consumed lots of power and generated lots of heat, and it failed far more regularly than the memories of today. The changes of memory technology in the last few years have improved the performance and price per byte of memory out of all recognition. Also memory access times have become shorter, and the packing density has increased to the point where what used to be whole boards worth of memory is now contained in just one chip. All these improvements have drastically changed the role of an operating system's memory manager component.

When computer memories were small and expensive, the mini computer designers of the day had two choices when it came to running a lot of users. First: do not. Run only those users who can be fitted into memory. Second: disk swapping. The concept of simple disk swapping is that you take the complete memory which is allocated to a user and write it into a file on your disk. This file is often called a swap or checkpoint file, and should be big enough to accommodate all the user jobs which are liable to be swapped into it. Any disk swapping system has a considerable impact on system performance — that is, the same system will run much more slowly performing the disk swapping to run more users. A user would be swapped out to disk when the memory which he occupies is required for another user. All the users of the system are swapped into and out of memory continually and they only make progress whilst actually in memory.

It might be a digression, but since the memory manager often initiates user swapping, this is perhaps a good place to look at the actual process of disk swapping, and later, in chapter seven, we shall see what it can do to the throughput of a system. Let us take the case of a DEC 11/04 processor. This processor can directly address 32KW of memory. It is an indication of ever hastening progression in processor design that almost every 8-bit microprocessor can now address this much memory, albeit organised as 64KB. The 32KW available using the 11/04 in our example has often been used to run RSTS V4. Where this is done the memory must house the following:

1) RSTS V4 operating system – including BASIC PLUS language. Size approx. 18KW. 2) 4KW allocated to memory mapped I/O for system devices. 3) Space for as many users as possible in what is left of the 32KW.

This allocation of the memory is shown in Figure 2.3. We see that after the memory mapped I/O and operating system have been located into memory we are left with 10KW of memory for the system users to run programs in. The most we could realistically expect to get into 14KW would be two users, allocated 5KW each. To anybody used to machine code programming or assembler programming this may sound like a lot, but as all high level programmers will know, it doesn't take long write a program which will occupy this much, and BASIC is often reckoned to be one of the less memory efficient programming languages. Therefore, 5KW may be OK for some simpler applications, but when anything more complex is required the space available to each of our two users will soon become restrictive. Since the system costs a lot of money, it may not be acceptable to give all user space to one user only; therefore some means must be found to allow the user memory space to be shared by several users. The only way of doing this which does not involve extra hardware – thus raising the cost – is user swapping. In a swapping scheme each user's program, and the data which that program is currently processing, are written into a special file on the system disk unit(s) whilst another user's program is read in from another part of the same swapfile. The net effect is that each user on the system has a set time in which his program is resident in memory (and is thus progressing). After expiry of this time the user is swapped out into the swapfile and another user is brought into memory from the swapfile. The new user now has a burst of memory residency (and CPU time) during which his job progresses. At the end of the residency time the next user is swapped

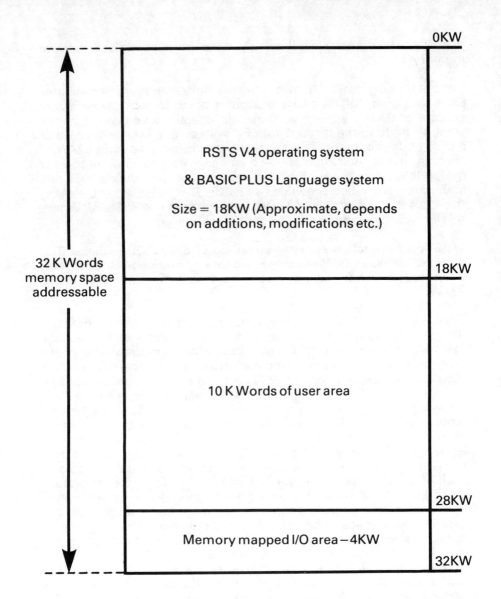

Figure 2.3   PDP-11/04 Memory allocation V4 RSTS

24

in from the swapfile whilst the current user is swapped back into it. All the users logged on to the system are swapped in and out in turn on a round robin basis. The swap process happens fairly swiftly, and each user may only be swapped out for less than a second. But conversely, each user is also in memory for a few milliseconds, so that when watching output from a program at his terminal, the user will notice that it appears in little bursts, with the time between each burst representing the time that the program is swapped out. The exact trouble spots in swapping will be examined in Chapter Seven, but suffice it to say for the moment that swapping out to disk is not a desirable feature where it is used in such a basic way as that just described. Fortunately, modern mini computers and operating systems have many times the amount of memory available to their predecessors, and although swapping is still widely in use, its use is more flexible and intelligent. Of course, machines still run out of memory to allocate to users, but the point at which this occurs is with far more users on the system. The memory manager initiates swaps, and the swapper carries them out. There are many new operating systems around which do not have any swapping capability. The advantages of this are that should it be required to take the system disks off line once the operating system has been loaded from them, there is no reason why this should not happen. Also, the operating system will generally be faster. The only drawback with no-swapping systems is that they have a definite limit on the number of users they can run; should this require expansion more memory will have to be purchased. Thus, where expandibility must be carried out at low cost, these no-swap systems are not an ideal choice when choosing an operating system.

The memory manager must provide sections of memory for use by operating system components and language systems. This often takes the form of a buffer pool. In the buffer pool method an area of memory is put aside for use as work area for the system as a whole. This area is split up into fairly small sections. When a request is received by the memory manager for a buffer it releases the address of one of these sections, which the requestor then has the use of. Prime consumers of buffer space are I/O drivers. For example, when a user sits at a keyboard typing in his commands, or other input, the characters typed are not examined or evaluated in any way until he types a terminating character — usually a carriage return. As each character is typed in they are placed into an input buffer. The memory manager released the use of this buffer to the terminal I/O driver as a result of the driver requesting a buffer when the user first began typing in. The terminal may receive output by the same kind of method. Characters to be output to a terminal are first placed in its output buffer – again provided from the memory manager's buffer pool. When the terminal driver sees that there are characters for sending to a terminal in an output buffer the terminal driver sends a character every time it finds the terminal's interface ready to receive one. The characters in the output buffer are put there as output from the user's program – e.g. a BASIC PLUS "PRINT" statement. When a user is not typing anything in, or there are no characters in his output buffer, the memory manager receives a signal that the use of the buffers are no longer required, and the buffers are returned to the free buffer pool. Many of the operating systems currently in use allow the size of the buffer pool to be specified by the person setting up the system. Getting the size right is very important, as if too small the system may hang up, with the world and his wife waiting for the memory manager to release a buffer in response to a request, while the memory manager may have none to release and no prospects of having any. On the other hand, the over large buffer pool may waste a lot of memory. In general, the latter is preferable as long as the waste is not too great, as there will be enough capacity to cope with peaks of buffer demand. Peaks occur because in real systems many buffers may be allocated per user, and in applications like word processing, where large amounts of text characters are input and output, the demand can be very erratic. Other demands on the buffer pool come from line printers, disks and magnetic tapes. Line printers, as mentioned in the section earlier in this chapter on I/O drivers, print a line at a time. The most common number of characters for a line of print on such a printer is 132. Since these are usually sent over a parallel data highway to the printer the transfer rate is high. Because there are a large number of characters being transferred from the computer to the printer its output buffer must be larger, to prevent wasteful repetition of fill and empty operations on the printer output buffer, midway through sending lines to be printed.

Disks dump data in blocks. Each block is large, and to aid disk transfer speeds the data is often dumped in multiple blocks. Consequently, large buffers are required. The same consideration must be applied to magnetic tape transfer buffering. The problem of balancing disk and magnetic tape multi-block transfers with excessive buffer consumption will be discussed a little later in Chapter Six.

Other general functions of the memory manager are to optimise users in memory. This includes moving them about when their size expands or contracts. The overall aim is to fit as many users as possible into memory, thus postponing swapping until the very maximum number of users are on the system.

With machines like the VAX, where very complex memory management is performed by hardware, the memory manager will have to set up that hardware to perform its function and maintain some degree of control of it. Also, in machines like the 11/34, the memory management registers must be set up correctly "on the hoof", so that as memory is allocated and relinquished each successive user of a part of memory has the correct settings of memory management hardware.

The memory manager may also have the capability to work around small parts of the memory which have been identified as faulty.

The memory manager, then, controls the allocation of memory to system components in need of buffers, it detects the need for and initiates swaps of user areas to disk, it dynamically re-locates users in memory as they expand or contract, and it might also report memory faults to the error logger in some systems.

2.4 Language Support.

Generally speaking, mini computers' users program in high level languages like PASCAL, BASIC, FORTRAN, etc. The bigger a machine is, the more likely it is to have more than one of the high level languages available. If each high level language had its own I/O drivers then not only would the operating system playing host be competing for access to system devices like disks or tapes, but the management of the file structure would be enormously complicated. In addition, a lot of needless duplication would take place. A far better and frequently implemented solution is that the language systems talk to the operating system as a kind of "add on" component, submitting requests to operating system components in a similar way to that in which the actual O/S components do. This method allows the programming language to be used for implementing system utility programs, where otherwise they might have to be built in to the operating system. This would result in a lot of redundant modules of the operating system being memory resident for much of the time.

Any language system will require a good deal of co-operation from its host operating system. For example, input from the user's terminal will be controlled by the operating system's terminal I/O driver. When the operating system detects a terminator typed at a terminal it may pass on the contents of the terminal's input buffer to the language system if it cannot resolve what the user typed into a command which it can recognise. The O/S may provide information about the system for use in programs written in the high level language. An example of this is the BASIC PLUS system string called "TIME $ (O)". This returns the current time from the operating system when used in the following format under RSTS: "PRINT TIME $ (O)". There are a great many examples of this simple interaction between the operating system and its languages, not only for BASIC PLUS, but for any other language which must generate terminal or printer output or fetch information from, or write information to system storage devices.

Whilst examining the support given by operating systems to high level languages it might be helpful to look at the kind of mechanism which programs can use to access or change system information. I draw this example from BASIC PLUS once again and it shows the kind of interaction which takes place with RSTS.

It is required for a BASIC PLUS program to find out some information about itself. The number of the terminal it is being run on, and the number the system has assigned to the job to uniquely identify it, for example. These things might be valuable for a program to know if, for example, the program must not be run from certain terminals for some security reason, where the user must have a message appear at his terminal which says, "terminal KB32: – job number 14". This information might be of value to the user when he wishes to arrange an interaction with another program which needs to know his terminal and job number. Within a BASIC PLUS program a mechanism called a SYS call (short for system call) may be used to pass information to or receive information from the RSTS operating system. The format of these calls is RETURNDAT=SPECDAT. This is to say, the RETURNDAT will contain items of returned data after the SYS call has been executed, and SPECDAT must contain the specification of what is required, and optionally data, before the call is executed. Where data is provided by the user program for modification of system values or parameters it must be in a strict format, since any digression from this format or illegal values will result in an error message. This has to be, since allowing such mistakes could crash the operating system. Character strings are used to pass the values mentioned above. This is possible because BASIC PLUS allows the use of a string of printable characters – for example, "ABC" - also to be treated as numerical values. The string "ABC" could also be used as ASCII numerical values which, in decimal, would be 65, 66, 67. The exact method of doing this is to use the CHR$(X) function common to most BASICs.

For example:

```
LET Z$=CHR$(65)+CHR$(66)+CHR$(67)
PRINT Z$
```

will give exactly the same result as:

```
LET Z$ = "ABC"
PRINT Z$
```

In the first case the numerical values are put in the string, in the second the text delimiters achieve the same result. When applying this to SYS calls we merely supply each byte of the SPECDAT string values laid down for the SYS call. For example:

```
A$ = SYS(CHR$(6%) + CHR$(26%) + CHR$(0) + CHR$(0))
```

The value 6% (the per cent sign signifies an integer as opposed to a floating point number) indicates that the SYS call is to the file processor; the value 26% specifies that we want the file processor to read our job statistics into the string A$. The two zero bytes tell the file processor that we want the first set of job statistics (RSTS keeps two sets per job), and that we want to read them, not change them. After this line of program has been executed the values of each byte in A$ will contain a value which the user's program can interpret and, if required, print out. Among other things this SYS call returns the following information:

1) the amount of CPU time so far consumed by the job since logging on to the system.
2) the number by which the system calls the job.
3) the number by which the system knows the user's terminal.
4) information about whether the job is swapped out (see section 2c).
5) the amount of time for which the job has tied up devices since logging on.
6) the program name.
7) the language support system's name.
8) the system account number to which the user is logged in.

This particular SYS call is used by the RSTS system utility program "SYSTAT", which shows details of all jobs currently running on an RSTS system. There is an entire DEC manual containing details of all the SYS calls and examples of the uses to which they can be put, but further examples are, I hope, not necessary, since the point is made that, using BASIC PLUS, a two-way interchange of information and parameters is available, which provides the language support facilities we have been looking at in this section.

The mechanisms for other languages under other operating systems may function in different ways on the face of it, but they mostly work on the same principle of providing arguments, data or parameters to an operating system component which is effectively called as a subroutine, and will return data about the system or its users.

2.5 The Job Scheduler.

A job scheduler is the operating system component which must share out the computing power of the CPU on as fair and efficient a basis as possible. In a multi user (or time sharing) system a number of users are connected, yet each must be unaware of the others to as large a degree as possible. This means that no user should interfere with another, and that each one should have the illusion that they are the sole user of the system. Given the immense computing power of modern machines this illusion is attainable where the number of users is not excessive, although in fact each user will actually progress in little bursts (i.e. during the time they actually run on the CPU). The frequency of these burst will, if the machine is not overloaded, look pretty much like a continual pogress. The actual component of the system which decides who is going to be next to have a runburst on the CPU is the scheduler. A very basic machine like that described in section 2.3 will have a job scheduler, though it will not need to be a very complex one, since it is really deciding who to swap in (in co-operation with the memory manager and the swapper) or out. This simple job scheduler is called a "round robin" scheduler. This is because the table of logged-in users is scanned in a round robin fashion, with no user being able to qualify for any extra CPU time, and every user being allocated his CPU time whether or not he can make use of it. This round robin scheduler has a number of glaring deficiencies chief of which is that it wastes CPU time, allocating as it does CPU time to even those users who cannot make use of it.

In order to become more efficient the JOB scheduler must be made more selective in whom it doles out bursts of CPU time to. This will mean the scheduler itself must be more complex and therefore larger and slightly more CPU consumptive. To be more selective the job scheduler must have information about what state each logged-on user is in. A few example states might be:

1) Ready to run on the CPU.
2) Completed all processing, now idling.
3) Waiting for input at the user's terminal.

4) Awaiting information from disk to be fetched, cannot proceed till then.

5) Awaiting service from some operating system component (often the file processor which may handle only one request at a time).

6) Awaiting access to some hardware device, like a line printer.

7) Awaiting free space in the terminal's output buffer — this can occur where the program puts information to be printed to a terminal into its output buffer and then waits till the output buffer has been emptied out to the terminal by the terminal's I/O driver.

8) Halted by error — some hardware function or program error has caused the user's progress to halt. Operator intervention is now required to resume/restart it.

For all these states, with the exception of (1), the allocation of CPU time would be pointless until some external event makes them change to the ready-to-run state. Consequently, any job not in state 1 can be ignored for the purposes of the scheduler, and further can be swapped to disk if it isn't waiting for disk I/O or the file processor, since the other states will probably take a relatively long time to change to ready. This type of scheduling will certainly be better than our round robin method, but it still lacks a further refinement which can be added to ensure that jobs requiring a rapid response get it, though at the expense of those jobs to which a rapid response time is less crucial. This refinement is of course prioritising. In this scheme every user when he logs on is given a priority level at which he will run, for as long as he remains logged on to the system, unless he deliberately changes it. Users with a higher priority are given a burst of CPU time more often than those with the lower priority. There are dangers in this kind of prioritising: mainly that one high priority user can effectively lock out all other users connected to the system depriving them of any CPU time whatever. However, this deplorable state of affairs is usually combatted by imposing, within the job scheduler, a time limit for which a ready job can be left without a burst of CPU time. Again, this makes the job scheduler yet more complex, but since most major multi user operating systems now use prioritising, the designers of operating systems must have found that the price is a fair one to pay for the advantages gained. The concept of prioritising will not be fully discussed here, but in Chapter six there will be an example of setting up correct priorities for different kinds of users. One final point — just so there are no misunderstandings — the priority levels mentioned here are nothing to do with the interrupt priority levels built into the computer hardware. The priorities mentioned here are purely internal to the operating system and do not alter or affect the hardware priority levels.

2.6 Command Interpreter.

When a user types in a command at his keyboard the command will almost always be a word or a group of words. Now as the computer understands only binary numbers, some conversion routine must be used to convert the words typed in to some form more readily understood. This function is performed by the command interpreter (sometimes called a command line interpreter or command parser). The function of the command interpreter is to compare whatever has been typed in at the system's terminals, or contents of command files, to a list of commands which it is set up to recognise. If it finds a match it will call into action those components of the operating system which implement the command. There are a few types of command interpreter and each has its own little rules which you must obey if you are to get it to understand you properly.

Many command interpreters will recognise abbreviated commands. Thus the command "COPY" could be abbreviated to "COP". RSX will, in the general case, allow abbreviation down to three characters. VMS will allow many commands to be shortened to just two. The rules of abbreviation are that a command may only be shortened as long as it does not become ambiguous by so doing. Thus the command "DI" could mean either DIRECTORY or DISMOUNT, so that would not be permissible. But the commands "DIR" and "DIS" would both be good. The interpreter must scan the valid command list and compile a list of probable matches for the command. If more than one probable is found, and none can be eliminated, then an error must occur. Commands to RSTS may not be abbreviated except using the CCL facility (see section of RSTS special features in appendix one).

People like engineers, who may transfer between several different operating systems and machines in the course of every day can find themselves not only typing the wrong commands for the system they are currently working on, but also getting the syntax and format of their commands rejected. The major differences between the command interpreters of the three operating systems used as examples in this book are their use of spaces and their methods of passing parameters to programs. The space character is used by VMS and RSX as a field separator, whereas on RSTS it is not. For example, if we type in the command "runtrek" to RSTS, the program "trek" will be run, but if we type the same to VMS and RSX they will issue an error message which says something like "illegal command "runtrek"". This is because they interpret everything in a command line up to the first space as a command (in this case, the command "run"), and everything that follows the first space to be parameters, filenames, or qualifiers (in this case the filename "trek"). The RSTS command interpreter will just look for a command which it recognises, and doesn't mind if there is a space or not after it. (This does not apply to RSTS CCL commands which must have a space after the CCL and before the parameters to the program which that CCL invokes). Let us look at another example of how the command interpreter looks at input commands. We desire – on a VMS system – to copy a file called "DISFILE.TST" to a new file which we want to call "DATFILE.TST", so we type in the command "COPY DISFILE.TST DATFILE.TST". In this case the command language is DCL (Digital Command Language), and everything up to the first space will be taken as a keyword. A keyword is a word which should appear at the beginning of a line of input. The keyword "COPY" is recognised and the VMS copy utility (which is used to transfer files rather than copy whole disks) is run. The command interpreter passes a pointer to the rest of the input, i.e. "DISFILE.TST DATFILE.TST", which copy will interpret as follows: everything up to the first space is the file specification of the file to be copied from, and the input after the first space is the filespec of the file to be copied to. Had the input been just the word "copy", the command interpreter would merely have responded with prompts to the user to obtain the names of the files to be transferred. A little finger trouble when typing in this command could completely alter the interpretation which the command interpreter and the COPY program place upon it. If we typed "COPY DISFILE.TSTDATFILE.TST" the command interpreter would correctly run the copy program, but copy would try to use "DISFILE.TSTDATFILE.TST" as a valid file specification, and the error "Illegal file specification" would occur – due to the missing space. VMS filenames are also limited to twelve characters. Likewise, if too many filenames were provided the command interpreter would pass them all to COPY. Then COPY would either ignore the extra ones or issue an error, "too many parameters" – type error message. These, then, are the kind of differences which must be born in mind when typing in commands to an operating system.

The way in which commands are actually recognised is very interesting, too. Many command interpreters will scan through a list of commands, comparing each to a list of valid commands until a match is found. However, the longer the list of commands which must be scanned becomes, the more time it takes to scan it, and a slightly more complex but faster method exists. In this method each entry in the list has a kind of checksum which is the total of all the ASCII values of the characters which go to spell it. For example, the command "RUN" consists of the ASCII values 82, 85 and 78. Total here is 245 (decimal). When a user types a delimiter into the system the command interpreter will add all the letters of his input up to the first space to get a checksum. Then only the checksum entries in the valid commands list need be compared until a possible match is found, then a full comparison is performed. The saving in execution time comes because in this method only those entries which are likely matches are actually scanned character by character. The disadvantage is that the valid commands list must be slightly larger to contain the necessary checksums. This method of command recognition is used extensively in the microprocessor field.

When language systems accept keyboard commands as well as their host operating system, the operating system's command interpreter must pass on to the language system unrecognised commands or input. The language system must then interpret the input and accept or reject it. If both operating system and language system fail to recognise the input then an error message must be issued. Then again, the command language may be given over completely to a programming language, and the operating system be given no front end at all, with all the operating systems functions being accessed via the programming language. This is the case with VMS, where the DCL command language is used for entry of all commands to the system (DCL is also used on the latest release of RSTS, where it is available as an alternative command interpreter and run time system to BASIC-PLUS). DCL can be used to write programs in the form of command files.

A command interpreter then takes the things you type in and sorts out what it is you want done, and then passes any relevant parameters which you supply to the operating system component or system program which implements the required action.

That completes our look at the major operating system components. I have not included here a comprehensive list, nor are the functional boundaries always as clear cut as I have here presented them. However, the foregoing should provide newcomers to the subject with a fair idea of what goes on inside operating systems. I hope that readers may be sufficiently interested in one or more of these components to find out more about them.

CHAPTER THREE
Breathing Life Into
The Beast

3.1 A Tug At The Bootstraps

We have just finished plugging in the last board on our newly constructed computer. We have connected the tape unit, the disk drives, some terminals, and now it is time to apply the power. With trembling finger we push the power switch to the "on" position, looking away as we do so. Then we look cautiously at the machine. No blue flashes, no smoke, no fault indicators...it works. Well, runs. We are now in the position that occurs every time a computer with a loadable operating system is powered on: we have a memory containing absolutely nothing. This is what software people term the "bare machine" or the "raw machine". We have a little bit of program in firmware, perhaps, whose purpose is to allow, examine and substitute operations on memory locations, and loading of programs from a disk or tape device. At this "bare machine" level the machine is practically useless for anything more complex than a little machine code programming, which has little to recommend it in terms of ease or speed. What we now require is to use our "load a program" facility to load a large program to run all our peripherals, cohesively manage our disk storage, format our terminal output, interpret terminal input, and so on. This large program is of course an operating system. The machine in question will have to have an operating system loaded into its read/write memory after every time it has been powered down. So why, given the increase in size and ease of use of modern read-only memory (ROM — whose contents are retained even with power removed) do many operating systems still have to be loaded into memory which loses its contents at every power-off of the machine? There are several advantages to having an operating system resident in volatile random access memory(RAM). For example:

1) The operating system can be altered (patched), perhaps with sections being deleted or added as required. Unlike ROM this will not

involve installing a new set of chips containing the new version, since using an editor or special patching program, the file on the disk containing the operating system can be edited like any other file.

2) Some processors are more efficient when they can work on areas of data which are adjacent in memory to the program being run. This is because the data address can be specified as an offset to the program counter. This will save a dedicated pointer to the data area and the program might also execute a little more quickly. Obviously, since the data area must be read from and written into, this could not be done with ROM.

3) Extensive use of overlays can be made. Overlays are infrequently used sections of an operating system which can be loaded in from disk as required, executed, and then the memory they occupy freed up as soon as execution completes. The advantage of this is that the overall size of the operating system can be reduced. Again, this would not be feasible in a read-only memory. The sections overlayed are the least used parts of an operating system, and if the facility is used wisely this has little noticeable effect on the system performance.

4) Various operating systems can be run alternately on the same machine. This is simply a matter of having all the required systems on different disks, and loading the one required. This is of great use to, for example, software maintenance offices, and that select band of users who use one operating system for some of their processing and another for the rest.

This process of loading a large program (an operating system, for example) under the control of a smaller program is called bootstrapping. The term bootstrapping is derived from the metaphor that the system is pulling itself up by its bootstraps. The bootstrap program (commonly abbreviated to 'boot program') simply loads a bigger program and thus, like Alice, the size of the loaded program(s) just grows and grows. We shall come to three accounts of bootstrap sequences later on, but now we will discuss the general implications of what has already been said on the subject.

If you are going to load in your operating system every time the machine has been powered down, you can initiate the load in two ways. First, you can have the machine owner or operator key in a small machine code program whose purpose is to load a more sophisticated boot program from a disk (or tape). This will, however, involve the person doing it in a lot of rather tedious work, and the process is hardly user friendly. Second – and most acceptable – method is the firmware method previously mentioned. A boot program is held in a small area of ROM. When the machine is powered on, the hardware forces the processor to begin executing the program in ROM, which will begin the boot process. Variants on this are that the program held in the firmware may allow a minimal dialogue wih the master (or console) terminal to permit the user to select which device the operating system is to be loaded from. (The PDP-11 uses this method, and can also be set up to bootstrap from a set device at every power-up). Another variant allows memory-or controller-testing from the firmware. This is a very desirable feature, but does mean that a larger amount of the available memory space is taken up by these ROM based programs. However, as memory spaces get larger this drawback becomes of less moment.

A very important implication of having a standard firmware bootstrap program, whose purpose is to load a secondary boot program from disk, is that the secondary boot program must be on a known position on the device from which it is loaded. The usual solution is to reserve the first data block of any "bootable" device for this secondary boot program. Thus, for disks sector zero of track zero, head zero will be used. And on tapes the first block of data after the beginning of tape (BOT) marker will be used. There is one problem with using this particular block on a disk, and this will be detailed in section 3.5 of this chapter.

Before examining the ways in which a boot program can fail, we will see how our three example operating systems are bootstrapped.

3.2 How VMS is bootstrapped.

VMS runs on DEC's range of VAX processors, and all of these have different front end devices, separate from the actual VAX processor. Because of this there is a difference in the initial stages of the bootstrap. But however different these initial stages are, the overall effect is to load a file – "VMB.EXE" – into memory address 200 (hex). VMB.EXE runs and sets up the processor registers, as the contents of these will be used as indicators to functions required/not required later in the boot process. VMB now searches for and locates, the file "SYSBOOT.EXE" on the selected disk, loads and runs it, passing parameters to SYSBOOT before terminating. Note that, at this stage, a different program called "DIAGBOOT.EXE" could have been loaded instead of SYSBOOT. This is used by engineers to run diagnostic programs rather than running VMS. The choice of which of the two to run is made by VMB.EXE, which bases the decision upon the state of the parameters it receives from the typed commands at the system's console terminal. A boot option allows a state called "conversational mode" to be entered. If this mode is selected the user is given a prompt from SYSBOOT upon receipt of which commands may be entered to change various system parameters before continuing with the start up of VMS proper. When the SYSBOOT program has completed setting up the system parameters it sets about loading the file "SYS.EXE". This contains the VMS operating system. If SYSBOOT is not in conversational mode there are no outward signs of its having run. It merely sets up default parameters and loads in VMS, which will have a ready made environment created by SYSBOOT. As a simple, machine specific, example of the exact sequence in which the VMS operating system is booted and started up, there follows a description of starting a VAX 11/750. The example details a conversational boot.

1) Power the machine on with the "power on action" switch in the "HALT" position. The machine now issues the console prompt consisting of three chevrons (>>>, known as the triple chevron prompt), and awaits a command.

2) Type in "B/10", and the machine now reads the state of the front panel "BOOT DEVICE" selector switch. This switch in effect selects one of four possible ROMs, each of which contains a boot program for a different device. The number after the "/" character is passed on to the VMB program, and later to either "SYSBOOT" or "DIAGBOOT", according to which is selected.

3) The boot program from the selected ROM now runs and sets about loading in the first block of the data from the selected device (commonly referred to as the boot block). The program contained in this first block is loaded into memory beginning at address zero.

4) The contents of the boot block (the secondary boot program – the ROM based boot program being the primary boot program) now run. The file "VMB.EXE" is now loaded into memory from the boot device, starting at memory address 200 (hex). "VMB" now runs, and creates a restart parameter block (RPB). This parameter block gives parameters to the next stage in the boot procedure. The exact contents of this RPB will be dictated by the type of bootstrap in progress and the value of the number after the "/" typed in with the boot command.

5) VMB now loads in the selected boot file SYSBOOT or DIAGBOOT into memory immediately above VMB. When the SYSBOOT program is used the RPB determines its exact run sequence. In this case we

have selected a conversational boot. SYSBOOT issues its prompt, then we may alter one or many of the parameters which will be used when timesharing begins under VMS. When we have done this we type in "CONTINUE", whereupon the SYSBOOT program locates the SYS.EXE file containing VMS.

6) VMS is now loaded. VMS performs yet more initialisations of the system (one of which is to enable the memory management features of the VAX). The VMS operating system now prints its name and version number on the console or master terminal and, if the machine has been powered down for some time, allowing the clock batteries to become discharged, then the user is asked for the date and time. The system services are now initialised and the system now goes multi user, with all the other previously inoperative terminal lines now responding to anything typed into them. VMS is now up and running.

VMS takes a relatively long time to get going because of all the work it must do in setting up a very complex set of hardware and a very sophisticated operating environment. The contents of the boot block on a bootable device may be rewritten or written for the first time using the "MCR WRITEBOOT" command, which will prompt for all the relevant information, rewriting the boot block after it has the information required to do so.

3.3 How RSX is bootstrapped.

RSX, in common with RSTS, runs on the PDP-11 machines, and is therefore bootstrapped in a broadly similar way to RSTS, at least in the initial stages of the bootstrap. RSX is bootstrapped in three identifiable stages. First the ROM-based firmware contained in an M9301 – or an M9312 or similar module – grabs the bus on power up and, depending upon how it is set up, either issues a prompt on the console terminal or sets about booting a device whose identification it establishes from the code set-up on a set of links and switches on the firmware card. If the prompt was issued the console user must type in a two letter code and unit number to indicate the type and number of the device he wishes to load the RSX operating system from. In both cases the firmware will now load in from the seected device the first block of the selected device, usually a disk. The first block of the disk contains a small program which has been set up to "know" where the file containing the RSX operating system is stored on the disk. This "primary boot" program is not large or complex enough to be able to search the disk directory for the file, so the command "SAV/WB" is used when RSX is actually running to rewrite the boot block on a disk, in cases where the boot block must be rewritten due to its being corrupted or the operating system file having moved on the disk. The boot block code will then boot in whatever it finds at the block where it thinks RSX should be, and if the file has been moved on the disk, accidentally deleted or corrupted, the boot block code has no recovery or error reporting capability. The RSX operating system is contained in a file which by default is called "RSX11M.SYS". This file is in the (0.0) directory and is usually 498 blocks in length, though this may vary according to the precise system specific arrangements. The file must be contiguous. The next step is that the boot block code loads in the first couple of blocks of the "RSX11M.SYS" file, which contain a larger, more comprehensive, bootstrap program. This primary boot program does a few more jobs, like enabling memory management, and then loads in the bulk of the rest of the file, which contains the RSX operating system. Control is then handed over to RSX, which performs its own initialisation and commences timesharing.

3.4 How RSTS is bootstrapped.

RSTS is bootstrapped in three main stages. First, the primary bootstrap program is loaded. Next the system initialisation program is loaded. Finally the RSTS operating system is loaded and takes control. Now we will examine these stages in more detail.

The primary bootstrap program is contained in the lowest numbered data block of a RSTS disk; it may also be contained in the data block of a tape nearest the BOT marker of the tape, but RSTS is only very rarely booted from tape for setting up a new installation from distribution tapes. The primary boot block is loaded under the control of ROM based firmware on a special module installed on the computer's backplane. This firmware may be automatically executed on power up, or the operator may type in the device code and number to be booted from at the system console. On some older PDP-11s there is no module containing firmware, and the operator may have to enter the boot program into the system's RAM memory and then start it executing – a tedious business. The program contained in the boot block – the primary boot program – now begins execution. It is loaded into memory beginning at address zero, but the first thing it does is to relocate itself to octal address 157000. This is in order that the lower part of memory is left clear for the next piece of software to be loaded. Once the primary boot program is relocated, it begins to load the file "INIT.SYS", which contains the initialisation program for the system. The primary boot program needs to "know" the exact whereabouts on the disk of "INIT.SYS", since it does not have the ability to search the disk directory for it. There is a RSTS system utility which allows the primary boot program held in the boot block to be rewritten, should "INIT.SYS" ever be moved to a new position on the disk. This utility is called "HOOK.SAV". The way in which the primary boot code loads in "INIT" makes no assumptions about the disk controller being one hundred per cent functional. It polls the controller rather than making it interrupt during this load. Only some parts of the "INIT" program are loaded; other modules of it will be loaded as required. Once "INIT" is in memory it begins to run. Its first action is to issue a bus reset instruction. This instruction will issue a hardware reset signal to all interfaces and controllers connected on the computer. Having ensured that all hardware is reset to a known condition, "INIT" now makes use of a DEC hardware feature: if any attempt is made to access an unoccupied memory address the processor can be forced to load the contents of the memory addresses 000004 into its program counter and then resume program execution from the new contents of the program counter. "INIT" now tries to access every valid I/O register address. If the address is populated, the program adds the address to a list called the "hardware list". This list is an invaluable aid to engineers trouble-shooting a new or rearranged system because it tells them if the controllers and interfaces are all present at the correct addresses. After compiling the hardware list, the program now sets up each controller it deems to be present to make each, in turn, generate an interrupt. The time each is allowed to perform this is not infinite, for the hardware clock is programmed to generate a timeout interrupt if the device has not interrupted within a fixed time limit. During an interrupt sequence on the PDP-11 the interrupting device must supply an interrupt vector address. Interrupt vector addresses are addresses supplied by the controllers or interfaces which point to two words in memory where the address of a software routine which will handle the interrupting device can be found. Thus it can be defined as follows: an interrupt vector is the address of the address of the interrupting device's handler. When the "INIT" program has ascertained the interrupt vector of each controller, this information is added to the hardware list. If any controller fails to interrupt within the time allowed for it to do so, "INIT" disables it and prints the message "DEVICE XX DOES NOT INTERRUPT- DEVICE DISABLED". After a few other checks, "INIT" prints the system name and version number, then the prompt "OPTION". The "HA LI" command merely lists out the hardware list which was compiled in the procedure detailed above. The "start" option begins getting to the stage where RSTS can be loaded and begin to run. After typing "start" (or just pressing the line feed key) on the console terminal the user receives messages about which devices the system expected to see but didn't.

These are not necessarily an indication of a fault, but more usually indicate that the operating system has the capability to run the indicated hardware, but that it is not present in the hardware configuration. This does not bother RSTS; it just carries on. Also during this phase the user receives a message indicating the maximum number of users which can be run (called JOBMAX) and the maximum size of the memory each user may occupy, called SWAPMAX. Next, the console operator is prompted for the date and time. Then "INIT" creates an initial environment for RSTS, and RSTS is loaded into memory, overwriting "INIT". RSTS now takes control, and begins by calling its own initialisation program – "INIT.BAC" - into action. This program prompts the user for a "COMMAND FILE NAME?". The user may type in just "carriage return" or the name of a file which contains commands for the setting up of the system to the requirements of its users. If just "carriage return" is pressed, a default command file "START.CMD" is executed. At the stage where RSTS takes control the system goes multi user, though, until logins are enabled, typing anything at any other terminal than the console will result in a "NO LOGINS" message being printed. Logins are authorised by a command contained in the startup command file.

3.5 Some general points about bootstrap or system initialisation failure.

It is probably true to say that the bootstrap stages are those which are most vulnerable to hardware failures or malfunction. This is because they are less protected by recovery procedures than an operating system in full flight. This has to be, since the very nature of a bootstrap program dictates that it be as small as possible. The cry "My system won't boot" is well known to people who answer calls at hardware maintenance companies. The most failure-prone aspects of the bootstrap will now be examined, and we will then look at our three operating systems and see the stages at which they might fail.

Earlier it was stated that the lowest numbered data block on the disk is used as the storage place for the primary boot program, but that this had disadvantages. The problem with using head zero, track zero, sector zero, is that if this block is corrupted or accidentally overwritten with rubbish, the bootstrap cannot succeed because the boot block is the sole link between the firmware (or manually entered) boot program and the subsequent stages of the bootstrap. So how likely is this block to be erased or corrupted? Let us take a case where the computer has been shut down; one of the last actions of the processor is almost certain to be issuing a bus reset instruction. This will reset all the controller and interface registers to zero. Now, having shut down the system, the careless operator powers off the machine before stopping the disk drives. When a processor – any processor, without auxillary power backup – has its mains supply removed, its electronics will generate all kinds of random signals for a very brief time. This phenomenon may be observed at many computer terminals: if they remain powered on during the instant that the computer to which they are connected to is powered on or off a spurious, random character will often be received by them. It is not unknown for the boot block to be overwritten, when a disk controller interprets one of these spurious characters as a write command, and has just enough power left to initiate the action on the drive. It must be remembered that the controller registers are all set to zero, so it is the boot block which gets overwritten by this mishap. The problem will mean that the next time anybody attempts to use the disk they will find that it does not bootstrap. The problem is well known to equipment designers, yet cannot be completely guarded against, on account of its random nature. The best thing is, of course, to tackle the problem at source and train the person performing system shutdowns always to shut off the disk drives before the processor. Also on the subject of block vulnerability, most, if not all, "hard" disk drives position their heads over cylinder zero when they first reach the correct rotational speed. The moment at which the disk heads are moved from their "off disk" storage position to load on to the disk is a fairly common time for them to come into light contact with the disk surface, as opposed to floating very close to it on a cushion of air – which is what they are supposed to do on most drives. This situation is normally rectified quickly as the cushion of air builds up. However, over a period of time this "load contact" can damage the recording surface of cylinder (or track) zero to the degree that it is not one hundred per cent reliable as a recording media. Cylinder zero, of course, contains our boot block. The above illustrates ways in which the contents of the boot block can be lost or made unreadable, but on the whole the boot block is comparatively rarely lost.

Assuming that our boot block has been brought into memory, its contents will now run and set about loading in some secondary boot program. Where can this fail? The boot block was located at the outermost cylinder of the disk, so we know that the disk heads did not have to be moved there from somewhere else on the disk surface. But now we almost certainly want to move the heads from the outermost cylinder to another one nearer to the centre of the disk. If we have some kind of servo fault on the disk head positioner, moving to a different cylinder will cause an error. If the primary boot program loaded in from the boot block does not have the capability to re-attempt this operation, the whole boot process will stall and die right away. A similar thing occurs when reading disks on slightly misaligned heads. The outer cylinders may be just readable, but the further towards the centre of the disk the heads try to read, the less likely they are to succeed. Again, this will cause an error to be generated which the primary boot program may not be able to handle. This marginal alignment problem also happens when trying to read a disk which was written when warm in a room where only the air conditioning has been on all night, and the disk has not been allowed to come back to a warm temperature, and therefore expanded ever so slightly. Many engineers have been called to sites where the system manager cannot get the machine to boot early one frosty morning, only to find that the now warmed-up disk boots perfectly. The remedy to this is to always ensure that at least fifteen minutes is allowed to elapse with the disk in the drive, but not spinning, to allow warming up before attempting disk copies or bootstrapping the system. On an exceptionally cold morning even longer may be required.

But assuming that the disk is functioning correctly and the secondary boot file is loaded, the next stumbling block is the system memory. The boot block code occupied only a small part of the memory, but the secondary boot program is liable to occupy a lot more. Assuming for the moment that the memory is not tested before the bootstrap commences, then if the secondary boot program is loaded into the faulty memory, the machine will appear to lay doggo. When this kind of thing occurs the most important thing to find out is, at what address did the machine halt, or what were the contents of the program counter when the processor was externally halted because it got stuck in a loop. We shall see in the next sections how important this piece of information can be. Memory testing prior to attempting a bootstrap is more likely to be implemented on a more recent machine, so as time goes on this kind of failure will hopefully become less common. Exhaustive memory testing does, however, take a long time, and cannot realistically be done prior to every bootstrap with X number of users impatiently waiting for the system to become available. Since electrical devices – be they logic circuits or light bulbs – most often fail at the moment of power on or power off, the bootstrap is the time these failures are first apparent – assuming they do not result in a total failure, in which case the bootstrap cannot even begin. In the case of a faulty interface or device controller, the worst things that can happen from a system point of view are that they can fail to interrupt or continually interrupt. These things can confuse, hinder or halt hardware initialisation procedure. When there is malfunctioning hardware present on a system at bootstrap time, the initialisation program should be able to cope with the most common failure modes, and inform the outside world exactly what the malfunction is. In the past, with earlier versions of some current operating systems, a system which failed to initialise properly also failed to indicate why. Current initialisation routines are more co-operative and can struggle on against errant hardware, and provide detailed information about a fault, saving downtime when the engineers arrive.

Now we shall take a look at VMS, RSX and RSTS, and suggest at which points the bootstrap of each might fail, and how one could accurately diagnose the reason for failure by applying the knowledge of the bootstrap sequence.

As already stated, the singlemost important thing to find out when a system fails to boot is the fail address (the contents of the program counter at the time the machine halted or was halted externally). This may often be found out from the printout provided when reinitialising the processor; in other cases it can be observed from the front panel display. Very often this information will enable an accurate assessment to be made of the point at which the failure occurred - which in turn should enable the possible causes to be narrowed down considerably. Let us elaborate on this a little.

The VAX processors provide an error code and a halt address when a bootstrap fails in its early stages. All that is required is to look up in the relevant manual the meaning of the error code and the cause can be isolated with a fair degree of certainty. Therefore a boot failure should be easy to diagnose.

RSX is not a very popular system with engineers because of its extreme sensitivity to hardware problems, and its relative lack of informational messages when it fails due to these hardware problems. If a device on the system is not included in the device list for a specific system, RSX will fail to complete its initialisation, yet not say why. This also applies when the system is up. If a hardware device for which RSX is not sysgened (a sysgen is a copy of an operating system specifically assembled for a particular hardware configuration), the whole system is liable to crash. Bootstrapping RSX may fail because a disk unit is totally inoperative, and the firmware cannot load in the boot block. Next it may fail because the boot block is corrupted, or as previously mentioned, because the absolute block number which the boot block code points to contains nothing, or a corrupted version of the "RSX11M.SYS" file. At any stage the boot may fail due to a faulty memory location causing the boot programs to be stored incorrectly. The boot block code when it runs away will almost certainly require a disk head seek, which might, if the disk servo has an oncoming or marginal fault, cause a seek error, which will make the boot block code fail. When the first blocks of "RSX11M.SYS" are loaded the next hurdle is the memory management. If this is faulty, and the fault is such that the memory management is inoperative, unpredictable results may ensue when it is used. Finally, it may happen that the first couple of blocks of the file containing the primary boot block are correct, but that some corruption exists in a later block of the file: this once again can halt the whole process of the bootstrap without any outward sign of why.

Diagnosing boot failures is really down to machine code programming to load in the boot block, then examining the disk registers to see if an error occurs. Next, machine code program a disk head seek, and once again see if the action produces any error. If all is well, use a small machine code memory test program to ensure that the first 32KW of memory is functional (only test up to 32KW because machine code programs to test above this will involve setting up memory management — depending on the machine — and that will probably increase the size of the program unacceptably when it has to be entered in machine codes). If all the memory tests successfully the next step is to see at what point the boot is failing. Perform a boot sequence and find out the contents of the CPU's program counter after the process halts. If the PC is an address in low memory the boot block code is failing. If, on the other hand, the address is higher in memory, the boot code is probably failing to load in the operating system. The obvious thing to do if no physical disk or head damage is found is to try another disk — but with it write-protected — to see if the boot sequence still fails in the same way, or merely because the disk unit is write-protected.

Now let us look at the RSTS bootstrap sequence and see what the fail address will tell us. The first failure could be that the system cannot load the primary boot block. A failure at this stage will result in a fail address within the address space of the firmware. (On the PDP-11 with the firmware contained on a 9301 or similar firmware card this will be an octal address beginning with 173XXX.) If the boot block was loaded in from the disk correctly, this does at least indicate a part functional memory/disk unit/disk controller configuration, but remember that the controller does not, at this stage, have to have a full interrupt capability since interrupts are not used until after "INIT.SYS" is loaded. Next the primary boot block relocates itself from address 000000 to address 150000. Any failure at this stage caused by faulty memory will show up as a trap to location 000004. Less likely, though still possible, is the case where the boot block was loaded with an undetected error which prevents the primary boot program from running correctly. This type of failure might result in a failure within the first 512 bytes of memory, or it may result in a random branch to any location in memory with the pocessor eventually encountering a "HALT" instruction at some completely unpredictable address. If you want to take a look at the contents of the boot block (by writing a small machine code program to load it into memory) to assure yourself that it does look like a boot block and not complete rubbish, load it in and examine the first two words of it. For a RSTS boot block these should be 240 (which is the PDP-11 machine code for a no-operation instruction (NOP)), followed by the value 525 as the second word. If these two values are correct it is a fair assumption that the block has at some time — perhaps still does — contain a valid primary boot program. Do not assume that because these two values are correct the boot block is intact, since there may be corruption of the block further on. This quick check will, however, serve to reassure you that you are not wasting your time attempting to bootstrap from a disk which contains no vestige of a boot program.

Assuming that the primary boot program has successfully relocated itself to address 150000, it now begins loading in the system initialisation program "INIT.SYS" from the booted disk. If at any stage in the loading of "INIT" there is a disk error, the primary boot program executes a halt instruction at address 157044. This will show as a fail address of 157046. This particular phase of the bootstrap fails most commonly, since up to this point the disk heads have not had to be moved, but "INIT" does not reside on cylinder 0; consequently this is the moment that all those nasty head positioner servo or marginal head alignment problems previously discussed will come into play. Another possibility for failure at this stage is a memory failure coming to light because "INIT" will naturally occupy (and therefore test) more memory than the primary boot program. Once "INIT" is correctly loaded the primary boot program hands control over to it. As previously discussed, "INIT" first polls the I/O address space to see what hardware interfaces and controllers are present on the system. The bus "INIT" instruction is used at the commencement of this process to ensure that the hardware will be in a known condition. This has the effect on many terminals of causing a spurious character to appear; often for printers this will be a hash character, or for VDUs it may be a light block or Tilde. Whatever character is printed, it is a useful indication that "INIT" has taken over and is running. "INIT" fails very seldom once loaded, though if there are faulty interfaces or controllers present it may take a long time to execute the hardware list compilation stage, and will print up messages to indicate the faulty hardware items before printing its prompt, "OPTION". The reason for this is that during the second stage of this hardware detect and test phase each of the present interfaces or contollers is set up to generate an interrupt, and thus the program will be unable to protect itself from an item of hardware which has a fault causing it to continually interrupt. The next critical point occurs after the "START" command has been given in response to the "OPTION" prompt, and the time and date have been entered. RSTS is now loaded into memory and takes control. This is the point at which timesharing begins, with the console terminal going from being polled to interrupt driven; thus, if the console terminal interface does not interrupt properly, the system will appear to die. Also at this point all the controllers and terminal interfaces are enabled to interrupt. When this happens any terminal lines which are permanently raising interrupts will occupy the processor on interrupt servicing to the extent that the rest of the initialisation cannot proceed, or will proceed extremely slowly. The system initialisation will only be completely halted by a rogue terminal line when that terminal is set to run at a high baud rate. But any problem of this nature will slow down the system initialisation considerably. This kind of problem is very often caused by long data cables being connected into the terminal interfaces with no terminal at the far end, causing the cable to act as an aerial, picking up random noise and feeding it into the computer as data. The solution is to keep all unused data lines disconected at the processor end. This problem is often the cause of a slow running system (see chapter seven).

3.6 Methods for isolating boot failures.

After tying down a bootstrap failure to a specific unit of the system, engineers will often try to diagnose the specific fault on a particular board. This will almost always involve some machine code programming – to make disk units do reads and seeks, or to run a check of memory for stuck bits, for example. A discussion of machine code programming is beyond the terms of reference set out for this book, but any interested readers can find titles for further reference in the bibliography, appendix four. Suffice it to say that with all our example systems – except the VAX - if you cannot load the operating system then you cannot load any ready-written diagnostic programs. This leaves the two alternatives of a wholesale swap of failed boards or units for functional ones, or some machine code programming to obtain the exact cause of a board or unit failure. The first of these two alternatives is the one most often taken, for the sake of minimum machine downtime.

CHAPTER 4
Introduction To, And Reasons For Having, File Structures

Any large amount of stored information, whatever method is used to store it, must be ordered in some fashion. If this were not the case it would be necessary to search from the start through till the desired piece of information was found. For example, in a large card index, which computer systems so often replace, all the cards are filed away in a logical order. Perhaps this may be in alphabetical order, or in some other order, such as transaction dates. In order to access an item in the card index users merely locate an entry which corresponds most closely with the one they require. One method of access is to find a card beginning with the same letter, or having a transaction date just prior to the one required. Then it is simply a matter of searching through the section until the item is found. I am sure that at some time readers will have had the experience of locating an item in such a card index. The only drawback to this system are that the bigger the data store becomes, the longer it takes to access an individual card, and of course the size of the area which the card drawers will occupy increases. The first drawback also applies to computerised storage of large amounts of data, though even a slow computerised data access will be faster by far than a manual system, the more so as the size of the stored data increases.

The information held on an average computer is not all of one type. There may well be a good deal of the type of information which the computer's owner had formerly stored in a card index. In addition there will also be other types of information. A prime example of this is a set of programs which the computer will run, to add to, alter or access the stored information. Then there is the computer's operating system, and all the system utility programs. Other information may be engineer's test programs and of course directories. It is important to realise that, as far as the operating system is concerned, there are only two types of information. First, directories: these are items of information which list the files on the system, along with information about those files. Second are the files themselves; files may contain data, programs, text or any other form of information which the computer is required to store. The operating system treats all files according to a set of rules, and broadly speaking does not care what kind of data is held in them.

The organisation of directories varies greatly between operating systems, but fortunately there are a number of similarities which we shall examine before we go on to look at a file structure in detail.

The term "file structure" is a blanket phrase which is used to describe the format in which directories and files are held on a computer system. The phrase is most often applied to file storage on disk units. The term "directory structure" is used interchangeably with "file structure".

As discussed in chapter three, the system needs to know where to find its primary bootstrap program. It must also know where the "front door" to its directory system resides. This first access point of the directory must be at a set location on a disk, or at least there must be a pointer to this first access point located at a known position on the disk.

Multi user system directories are usually organised in a tree structure, starting from a single root point and spreading out through all the various branches (sub directories). The root, or master, directory is stored at a set point on the disk, mostly in a set block number of the disk, although the boot block can sometimes contain a pointer to it. This root directory contains a table of all the directories which reside at the next level to it, their locations on the disk, and perhaps some other information to locate files which are stored on the system, and they may also contain pointers to yet more directories residing on a third level. The root directory is, then, the entry point to any file access, providing the access information to the next order directories and ultimately every file on the system. So long as the root directory is in a known position, the directories which follow on can be located anywhere on the disk. We illustrate this overall concept in Figure 4.1.

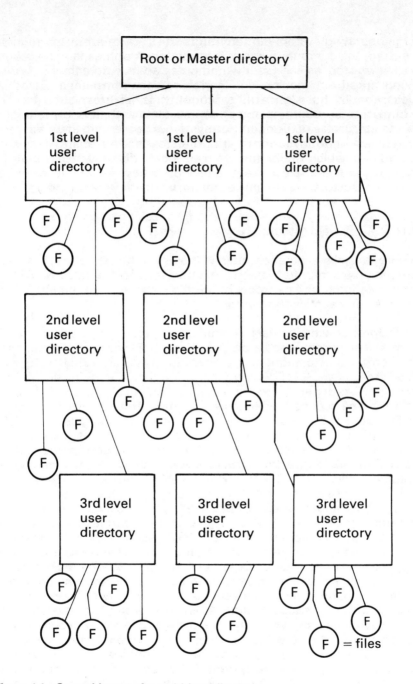

Figure 4.1   General layout of a multi level directory

If the operating system did not impose a structure for file storage on a system the computer's storage and fast retrieval capabilities could well be wasted, as each user would worry about where their data was being stored, and inevitably each would try to impose their individual ideas about what standards to adopt, thus destroying the idea of information portability between like systems and probably resulting in, at best, a very random allocation of disk space, and at worst, total chaos, with nobody's information safe. Added to this, the system would be usable only by people with a very detailed idea about the system hardware, since each user would have to talk in terms of cylinders, sectors, etc., when specifying where to store their data.

4.1 RSTS File Structure in Detail

Before we take a detailed look at the RSTS file structure, it would probably be useful to those readers not familiar with using RSTS to introduce the broad concepts of the file storage arrangements used, and the other applicable features.

RSTS (pronounced Ristus) is a multi user operating system from DEC, and is usually regarded as one of (if not THE) most widely installed mini-computer operating systems in the world. The RSTS file store consists of a two-level directory structure. The hierarchically highest level consists of a single root directory called the Master File Directory, or MFD. The second level consists of many User File Directories, or UFDs. Unlike many other operating systems (UNIX, for example) these UFDs cannot contain any further links to yet lesser order directories in the tree structure. The MFD, then, constitutes the highest level in the RSTS directory structure, while the UFDs form the lowest and only other level. The entries in the MFD can relate to either files or UFDs, with entries which describe a file being only slightly different from those describing UFDs. UFDs, however, contain only information relating to files. Unlike many operating systems, for example RSX, a file stored on an RSTS system can only have one directory entry in one directory; multiple directory references to the same file are not permitted. Another concept of RSTS is that users log into the system using account numbers (not account names), and once logged into a particular account the account's UFD remains the default directory. Accounts and UFDs are indisolubly linked, so that if a user logs into account 44,100 his default directory will be [44,100]. This brings us to the subject of account/UFD identification methods. All the directories are known by a pair of numbers, separated by a comma, with square brackets around the figures to denote a directory. Each UFD and the MFD have a pair of numbers to uniquely identify them. The MFD, for example, is always known as [1,1]. Account and directory numbers may be in the range [0,1] through to [254,254]. The [1,2] UFD always exists on a RSTS system, and is used as the system library, containing all the Commonly Used System Programs (CUSPS), that is, the programs used by the system manager on a day to day basis for system monitoring and maintenance. Another account directory which always exists is [0,1]. This contains things like the system initialisation program "INIT.SYS" which we met in chapter three, and also the file containing the operating system. Also in the [0,1] account directory we shall find the language system libraries, and maybe some engineer's stand alone diagnostic programs.

RSTS imposes certain restrictions on file names. The file naming convention is that a six-character name is followed by a three-letter extension name, with the two fields being deparated by a dot. The allowable characters in file names and extensions are limited to upper case A – Z and numerals 0 – 9, plus the dollar and full stop characters. This limitation is imposed because the filenames are stored internally in a compressed format known as RADIX-50. This allows three characters from this limited character set to be stored in one 16-bit word. The extension name should convey the type of information in the file; for example, an extension of ".TXT" would signify that a file contained ASCII text, while an extension of ".LST" might indicate a file containing a listing. The system enforces the extension names ".BAC" for files containing compiled BASIC programs, and ".BAS" for files containing BASIC source programs. These are enforced as defaults, but may be overridden. Other than these, filenames may be whatever the user chooses, subject to the restrictions already mentioned. Each account has a password which must be correctly entered before the user is granted access to the system facilities. These passwords are held in the directories. Each file stored on the system has a protection code which states who is allowed to access or alter it. Accounts having a first number of one (e.g. [1,4]) are privileged accounts and users logged into them are allowed freedom of access to the more sensitive system facilities (displaying passwords of accounts other than the one they are logged into, for instance). Statistics are kept for the usage of time and system resources by users of each account, and the information is stored in the UFDs for examination by the system manager's program "MONEY.BAC". This is naturally useful to people renting out time on their machine.

Finally in this potted RSTS primer we come to the subject of variable cluster sizes. A cluster is a group of disk blocks grouped together and treated as one "super block". RSTS allows clusters to be 2,4,8, or 16 blocks long. All blocks in a cluster must be adjacent (contiguous), and

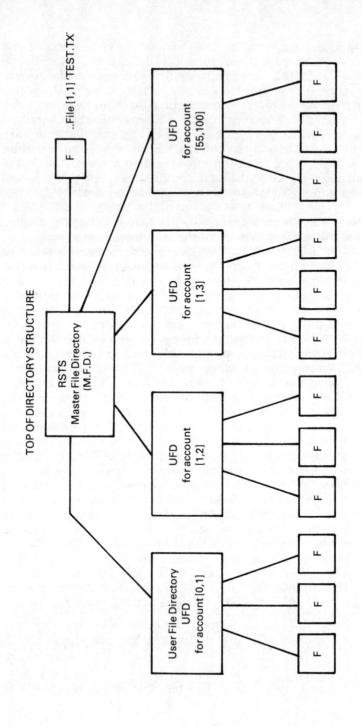

Figure 4.2 RSTS overall file directory information

Access to a file is via the MFD through the UFD. Note the file 'TEST.TXT' which is included to illustrate the fact that information held in the MFD can relate to UFD's or files stored in the system account 1,1. Unlike many operating systems RSTS UFD's cannot contain pointers to yet lower order subdirectories.

it is from this that the benefit of using clusters mainly derives. The subject will be explored more fully in section 4.3 of this chapter, when the whole question of disk optimisation will be examined.

The RSTS file structure is illustrated in block diagram form in Figure 4.2.

We will now examine the RSTS file structure in detail, starting at the top: the MFD.

RSTS uses a tree structured directory structure, as described in the previous section. The directory at the top of this structure is the MFD. The MFD (Master File Directory) is always located on disk at cluster one on a RSTS structured disk. Although the MFD always begins at cluster one it is not limited to one cluster in size. Further blocks may be added as required, although these subsequent clusters may be anywhere on the disk. This is because each cluster contains a link to the one following it. Therefore the first MFD cluster is the only one which has to be in an unvarying position on the disk. It is up to the software handling the directory management to detect when a link references a part of the directory not currently present in memory, and to cause the transfer of the required section of the directory into memory. Each directory block is, of course, 512 bytes, or 256 words long. The software treats these 256 words as 32 blockettes. A blockette here is defined as eight words. The types of blockettes are as follows (each blockette type will be detailed afterwards):

Label blockette
Name blockette
Accounting blockette
Attributes blockette
Cluster map blockette
Retrieval information blockette

Each of these blockettes will now be described, starting with the Label Blockette:

Label Blockette

No matter if the label blockette is for a UFD or for the MFD, the label blockette is always the first blockette in the first block of a UFD or the MFD. Figure 4.3 shows the format of the label blockette for the MFD and UFD, and although the contents differ after word four the similarity is obvious. Word one in both cases is a link (see links section) to the first name blockette in the directory. Word two is always set to

Content Description	Word
Link to the first name blockette of this MFD	1
Always set to minus one (all bits set)	2
Always zero (all bits clear)	3
Always zero (all bits clear)	4
Pack cluster size (minimum cluster size)	5
Pack status word – seven bit flags. See text	6
Pack ID. First three characters (Stored in RAD50)	7
Pack ID. Last three characters (Stored in RAD50)	8

Figure 4.3a   Label Blockette MFD

Content Description	Word
Link to the first name blockette of this UFD	1
Always set to minus one (all bits set)	2
Always set to zero (all bits clear)	3
Always set to zero (all bits clear)	4
Always set to zero (all bits clear)	5
Always set to zero (all bits clear)	6
Treated as two bytes each containing one number of the account number	7
Contains the text 'UFD' in RAD50 format	8

Figure 4.3b   Label Blockette UFD

minus one (all bits set), whilst the following two words are set to zero. These three words are useful as indicators to interrogating software that a RSTS file structure exists on the disk. In the case of the UFD label blockette the next two words are also zeroes. The word following these is treated as two bytes containing the account number which the directory represents (see RSTS description section). The final word – word eight – in a UFD name blockette contains, in the compressed RADIX 50 format, the text "UFD" to aid in identifying UFD blocks during attempts to rebuild a shattered file structure. The fifth word in an MFD name blockette contains the pack cluster size (see previous section on RSTS concepts). Word six of the MFD name blockette is a collection of flags called the pack status word. The bits within this word have the following functions and meanings:

Bit	Function
15:	Set = disk has been mounted (i.e. allocated for use). Clear = disk is not mounted.
14:	Set = the disk is public (i.e. may be used by any user). Clear = the disk is private (may have restrictions on usage).
13:	Must be clear.
12:	Must be clear.
11:	Set = the date shown against each file in directory listings will be the date that the file was last accessed. Clear = the date shown against each file in directory listings will be the date upon which it was last updated.
10:	Must be clear.
9:	Set = newly created files will be the first entries in the disk directories. Clear = new files will have directory entries added at the end of the directory.
8 through 0:	Must be clear.

Name Blockette

The name blockette differs considerably between its UFD and MFD version; accordingly the two formats for the name blockette will be described separately.

57

Content Description	Word
Link to the next name blockette in the MFD	1
Treated as two bytes containing the account number	2
First three characters (in RAD50) of account password	3
Last three characters (in RAD50) of account password	4
Treated as two bytes – high byte = protection code, lower byte = status flags – see text	5
Access count – number of users of this account	6
Link to accounting blockette for described account	7
Device cluster at which first block of UFD resides	8

Figure 4.4a   Name Blockette MFD

Content Description	Word
Link to the next UFD name blockette	1
File name (First three characters in RAD50)	2
File name (Last three characters in RAD50)	3
File name extension – three characters (RAD50)	4
Treated as two bytes – high byte is protection code, low byte is file status byte – see text	5
File access count, number of users using this file	6
Link to the accounting blockette for this file	7
Link to the retrieval information blockette	8

Figure 4.4b   Name Blockette UFD

The MFD format for a name blockette will be described first. In an MFD the name blockette contains information about a user file directory (UFD). Word one contains a link to the first word of the next name blockette; as with all other links, if this is zero then there are no more name blockettes in this particular directory. Word two in the MFD name blockette contains the number of the account UFD which the name blockette describes. All this is held in the format shown in Figure 4.4a. Words three and four contain the password to the account, six characters stored in RADIX 50 format. Following that, in word five, comes the protection code (high byte) and then the status byte (low byte). The protection code is not really a lot of use in an MFD name blockette, but is used in the UFD version. The status byte is a collection of flags used as follows:

Bit   **Function**

7:             If set, indicates that the file (or UFD) described by this
               name blockette is marked for deletion.

6:             If this bit is set, the name blockette describes a UFD,
               rather than a file.

5:             If set, indicates that the UFD or file described is not
               allowed to be deleted.

4:             Always set to one in the MFD version.

3:             If set, shows that the file (or UFD) is currently open in
               update mode.

2:             If set, the UFD or file is open for write accessing.

1:             If set, shows that a file is placed.

0:             In the MFD name blockette this bit is always set to zero.

Word six of the MFD name blockette contains the access account, which is the number of users currently logged into this account. Word seven is a link to the accounting blockette for this account. Finally, the last word in the name blockette of the MFD (word eight) is an absolute pointer to the location on disk of the first block of the UFD. Now we shall detail the contents of the UFD version of the name blockette – refer to Figure 4.4b. Word one is, as before, a link to the first word of the next name blockette in this UFD. Words two and three contain (in RADIX 50) the six characters of the name of the filename of the file which the name blockette describes, whilst word four contains the three-character extension name – again in RADIX 50. Word five is split into two bytes. The high byte is a protection code; its value describes the users allowed to access, update or delete the file. Bit seven, if set, specifies that the area occupied by the file is to be overwritten with zeros if or when the file is deleted – a data security feature. The status byte is the low byte of word five. The usage of the bits in the status byte is as detailed in the section on the MFD name blockette, excepting that bit zero, if set, indicates that the file is spread over this and another disk, and bit four, if set, indicates that a file is contiguous (see glossary). Word six contains the file access count, and indicates the number of users who are currently accessing the file described by this name blockette. Word seven is a link to the accounting blockette. Finally, word eight is a link to the first retrieval informaion blockette for this file.

Accounting Blockette

Once again, the formats of this type of blockette are different between the MFD and UFD versions, and accordingly will be detailed separately. See diagrams 4.5a and b.

The MFD accounting blockette, to begin with, at word one must have bit zero set and bits one to three clear. The rest of word one forms a link to the attributes blockette (if one exists for the UFD), as with all directory links. If zero, there are no further blockettes. Word two forms the least significant bits of the count of CPU time consumed by users of the UFD described by this blockette. Word six (high byte) is the upper eight bytes of this 24-bit count. The CPU time consumed is expressed in tenths of seconds. Word three is the time that the users of this account have been logged into the account, expressed in minutes. Word four is the lower sixteen bits of the accumulated kilo core ticks, or KCTs. One KCT = the usage of 1K of system memory for one second. The upper eight bits of this 24-bit KCT count are in word six of the MFD accounting blockette. Word five is the 16-bit count of the number of minutes which users in this account have had system devices assigned exclusively to them for. Word six has already been explained. Word seven is the number of disk blocks which the users of the account are permitted to retain when they log out. If the users of the account have too many blocks in use when the system LOGOUT program comes to log them out, they are not allowed to exit from the system until they have deleted some files, in order to get below the number of blocks indicated. Finally, word eight is the number of blocks in each cluster of the UFD.

Content Description	Word
Link to attributes blockette for the described UFD 0 0 0 1	1
Least significant 16 bits of accumulated CPU time	2
Accumulated time (Mins) users have been logged in	3
Accumulated KCT's — (see text) least significant 16 bits	4
Accumulated device time (minutes)	5
Treated as two bytes. High byte is most significant 8 bits of CPU time, low byte =MSB's of KCT's	6
Logout disk block count — see text	7
UFD clustersize — see text	8

Figure 4.5a   Accounting Blockette MFD

Content Description	Word
Link to files first attributes blockette 0 0 0 1	1
Date of last access/modification of this file	2
Number of blocks in file described (lower 16 bits)	3
File creation date	4
File creation time	5
Always set to zero	6
Treated as two bytes: upper byte is always zero, lower byte is upper eight bits of number of blocks	7
File cluster size	8

Figure 4.5b   Accounting Blockette UFD

And now to the UFD accounting blockette. Refer to figure 4.4b. Word one is used identically to the MFD equivalent. Remember that the accounting blockette in the UFD is for a file. Word two, depending upon the choice selected, contains either the date that the last access to this file occurred, or the date it was last modified. Word three in the UFD accounting block is the lower sixteen bits of a 24-bit value indicating the number of blocks of the file; the upper eight bits of this value are found in the lower byte of word eight. Word four contains the date on which the file was created, word five contains the time. Word six is a zero, as is the upper byte of word seven, whilst the lower byte of word seven has already been detailed. Word eight contains the file cluster size. The file cluster size can be equal to, or greater than, the disk cluster size (as detailed in the MFD label block). A file cluster size larger than the pack cluster size is advantageous when dealing with large data files.

Attributes Blockette

The attributes blockette applies to files, and is effectively a list of values indicating things like the number of the first and last block of the file, the record format used for data storage within the file, and so on. Figure 4.6 shows the details of the attributes blockette layout, but the fine details need not be listed, since they are not essential to understanding the concepts being presented here.

Cluster Map Blockette

Both the MFD and UFDs have as the last blockette of each block a cluster map. This is a list of the numbers of the clusters allocated to the directory, and saves searching through from the first block of the directory when a particular block of it must be accessed. The cluster map blockette is shown in diagrammatic form in diagram 4.7a.

Retrieval Information Blockette

This blockette, used only in the description of files, is a list of the absolute locations on disk of the blocks comprising a file. Retrieval blockettes are chained together by the use of the first word, containing a link to the next RIB in sequence. Figure 4.6b illustrates this. A link of zero indicates that it is the last RIB.

Finally, unused blockettes have words one and two set to zero to flag them as spare.

Content Description	Word
Link to next attributes blockette (if any)	1
Record format/file organisation/print control flags	2
Record size	3
Highest virtual block number (most significant 16 bits)	4
Highest virtual block number (least significant 16 bits)	5
End of file block number (most significant bits)	6
End of file block number (least significant bits)	7
Offset to first free block in EOF block	8

If a second attributes blockette is used the word numbers are continued into it.

2nd Attributes blockette for file description	Word
Number of bytes in fixed control area (VFC) =HI byt bucket size is in low byte	9
Maximum length of record (for RMS)	10
Default amount to extend file by when extend done	11
NOT DEFINED	12
NOT DEFINED	13
NOT DEFINED	14
NOT DEFINED	15
NOT DEFINED	16

Figure 4.6   Attributes blockette UFD

Contents description	Word
MFD or UFD Clustersize	1
Device cluster number (DCN) of first cluster	2
DCN of second MFD or UFD cluster	3
DCN of third MFD or UFD cluster	4
DCN of fourth MFD or UFD cluster	5
DCN of fifth MFD or UFD cluster	6
DCN of sixth MFD or UFD cluster	7
DCN of seventh MFD or UFD cluster	8

Note that a directory cluster map shows that the maximum number of clusters which may be in a directory is seven. Therefore the RSTS directory UFD's and MFD are limited to (7 times the pack cluster size) in length.

Fig. 4.7 Cluster Map Blockette MFD & UFD

Contents description	Word
Link to the next Retrieval blockette (if any)	1
DCN of cluster n+0	2
DCN of cluster n+1	3
DCN of cluster n+2	4
DCN of cluster n+3	5
DCN of cluster n+4	6
DCN of cluster n+5	7
DCN of cluster n+6	8

Fig. 4.8 Retrieval Information Blockette (RIB) UFD only

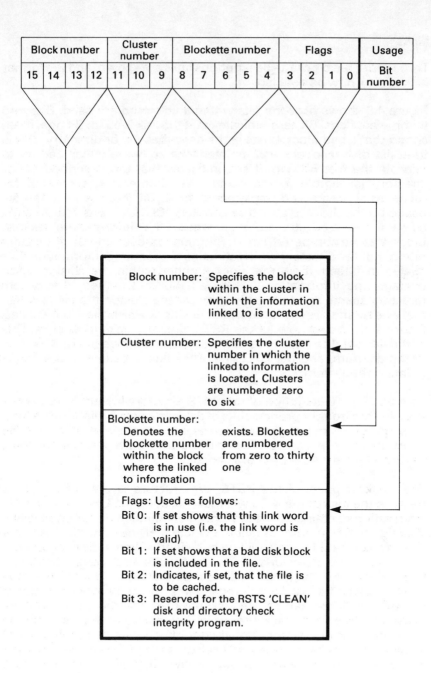

Figure 4.9   Layout of the RSTS directory Link word

Links

Throughout the blockette descriptions links are shown, and the format of these will now be detailed.

Figure 4.9 shows how the bits within a link word are used. Bits zero to three are flags. Bit zero indicates that the link is valid. Bit one, if set, shows that a bad block exists in the described file or directory; this is to assist disk recovery and maintenance software which can try to relocate the file. Bit two, if set, indicates that the described file or directory is eligible for cacheing (see chapter six, section B for cacheing concepts and implementations). Bit three is reserved for usage by the disk file structure checker, "CLEAN". Bits four to eight contain the blockette number where the information resides; blockettes are numbered 0 to 31. Bits nine to eleven contain the cluster number of the directory which contains the required information. Bits twelve to fifteen show the block number within the cluster which contains the information. Taking all this information, the system directory search software can establish: the cluster, the block within that cluster and the blockette within the block which the link indicates. Figure 4.8b shows how all the RSTS directory links interrelate. One particular point to note here is the single line between the MFD side of the diagram, and the UFD side. This illustrates one of the fragile points of the system.

So much for a description of the RSTS directory layout. Now we will examine the trouble-prone points of this particular directory structure, then go on to more general appraisal of the ways in which the directory structure can be affected by hardware when it malfunctions, or purely by the hardware characteristics.

The weakest point of the RSTS file structure is the MFD. This is because the loss of the MFD will make locating the UFDs, and the file information contained in them, extremely difficult, if not impossible. (See figure 4.8) In point of fact the whole MFD need not be lost – the loss of the label blockette will be sufficient! When a disk is mounted – i.e. when the system adds it to its list of available devices – the mount bit must be set in the MFD. This requires that bit 15 in word six of the label blockette be set. To accomplish this, the first block or cluster of the MFD must be read off the disk into memory, the bit set, and the revised block written back into place. Any failure of the disk unit, the memory, the processor or the disk controller during this operation will result in the disk being rendered useless, as the MFD will be unusable. Hardware errors which occur during rewriting UFDs after they have been updated usually result in the loss of some or all of the files which

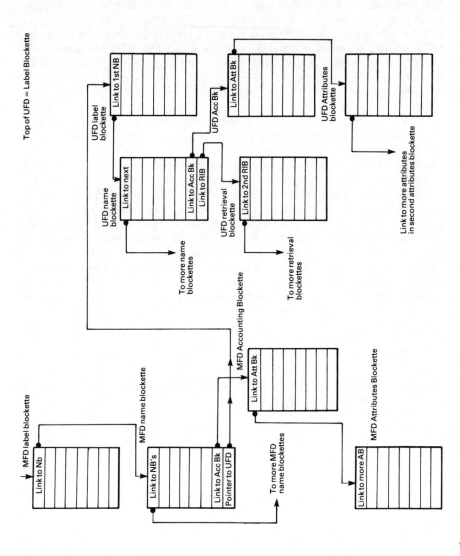

Figure 4.10 Inter-connection of RSTS Directory Blockettes

67

reside in the relevant account. If the directory links within a UFD are corrupted in such a way as to form a loop – this is, all the links point to other links – there is no last link, so a directory search will go on forever. This is a frequent reason for a system hanging up. Briefly, what seems to happen is that a UFD gets written to disk badly with a directory link corrupted. The next time a user accesses that directory UFD the file processor sets about searching the UFD for a required entry, and searches round and round the never-ending loop of links. The danger here is that other users will enter the file processor request queue and wait for the file processor to complete this directory search, which will never happen. I have been present to observe several of these kinds of fault. At least one turned out to be a faulty disk coating being sensitive to certain patterns altering crucial bits in a directory.

More generally, directories on any system are in constant use; indeed, they are the most frequently accessed item of data on the average system. Accordingly, the disk heads – can be floating over the root or user directories during idle times, and if any slight disk-to-head contact is taking place, it is liable to be the areas of the disk containing the directories that are most degraded. Indeed, there is at least one operating system which, because of this very point, positions heads at the innermost cylinder on its drives during times when nobody is accessing the disks, thus ensuring that almost all the data area will wear in step with the directories. Generally, then, the directories can easily be corrupted by the hardware if it malfunctions. Operating systems can make use of hardware features to guard against this, such as write check features on more intelligent disk controllers to make sure that what actually gets written on the disk matches what was meant to be written. Systems using controllers not possessing this checking capability can perform the check themselves by re-reading directory blocks after updating or modifying them, though in both cases there will be some overhead which will affect system performance adversely. In section 4.3 of this chapter the combination of badly maintained directories and how they can cause hardware "thrashing" will be examined.

4.2 Other Methods of File Structuring

The file structure used by the VMS operating system is a later version of that used by RSX. It is called ODS2 (RSX uses ODS1). ODS stands for Online Disk Storage. In ODS the root directory is not fixed in position as was the case with RSTS. The root directory is pointed to by an entry in the "Home Block". Thus the root directory is to be found anywhere on the disk. The Home Block, if lost, loses not only the location of the root directory but also the mount and pack status information for the disk. To combat this, there are several copies of the Home block at different locations on a VMS disk. ODS2 is a multi level structure and allows for sub directories to be held like files in directories which reside one level closer to the root directory.

This multi level concept allows there to be a number of different directory structures existing on the same physical disk unit. The advantages of this are that users' files can be segregated completely from one another, with only the system manager being aware that there are parallel file structures existing. This can only improve security between users, and can also help prevent cases of directory fragmentation from affecting such a wide number of the system users. Another purely hardware consideration is that the separate directory structures would probably result in more disk accesses on a system which handled its directory cacheing less efficiently than VMS. However, VMS - partly because of the increased memory available on most VAX machines when compared to their PDP-11 cousins, and partly because of the design philosophy of VMS – provides a very efficient implementation of this feature, which is beneficial to both system security and throughput.

With VMS there is a DCL command, "ANALYZE/DISK STRUCTURE", which can be used to look through the system directories and fix any part of them considered to be out of format, corrupt or suspect. Things like file dates and statuses are checked. This can be very useful as, unlike many directory checking utilities on other systems (e.g. the RSTS "CLEAN"), the VMS "ANALYZE" utility may be used online, and corruptions or format faults found in directories by "ANALYZE" are only fixed on the orders of the system manager. When the file structure of VMS is used properly it is a very efficient one, but it can become – like any file structure – fragmented. Fragmentation can be fixed by a total recreation of the disk directory structure, or simply by use of supplied programs, purpose-written to perform file structure maintenance. In the next section we shall look at this problem of fragmentation.

4.3 File Structure Maintenance

Where disk space is allocated and relinquished in a controlled but random fashion, there will come a time when the available free space will become fragmented. This fragmentation problem also applies to system directories and files which are frequently extended or contracted. The process by which disks can become fragmented is probably best illustrated by an example. To illustrate this we shall take a very simplistic view of a disk. Our simple disk has only one recording surface split into two tracks, each of which is subdivided into eight sectors. Therefore our theoretical disk will have a total of 16 blocks. Figure 4.11 shows this arrangement.

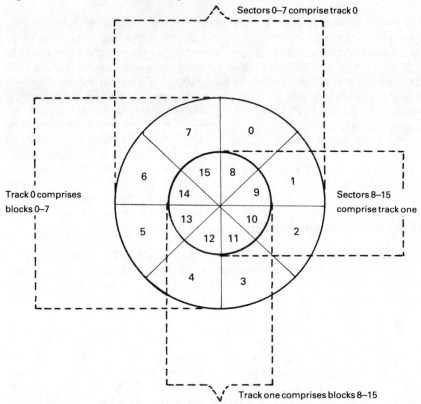

Simple disk with one surface, two tracks containing 8 sectors. Giving a total of sixteen blocks available for data storage.

Figure 4.11   Disk layout for disk fragmentation example

We reserve track zero, block zero for the directory. We join the action with files A and B already created on the disk. File A is five blocks long, whilst File B is only four blocks. The system user, after due consideration, decides that program A could be made to do all singing as well as all dancing, and accordingly adds to it, causing the operating system to extend file A by two blocks. This leads to the arrangement shown in Figure 4.13. Not satisfied with the upgrade to program A our maniac user, flushed with success, decides to perform a similar miracle on program B, and for good measure creates a new

70

Figure 4.12   **Figure 4.13**

Create files A and B

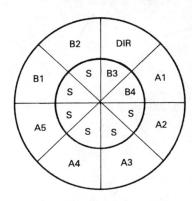

A1 = file A block one
B4 = file B block four ...etc.
S = spare block

Extend file A by two blocks

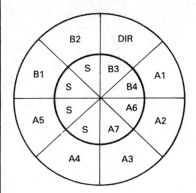

Extend file B by 3 blocks and create file C — one block in length. Disk now full.

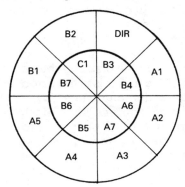

Delete file B, and extend file C by one block. Now there six spare blocks on the disk.

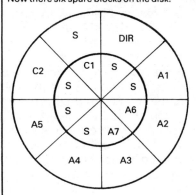

Figure 4.14   **Figure 4.15**

Create file D — four blocks in length. There are now three files on the disk, none of them is contiguous. There now remain only two spare blocks. The disk is now fragmented.

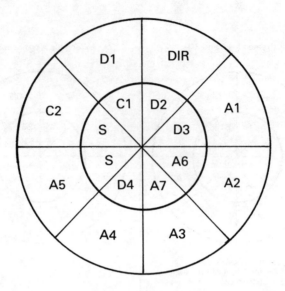

Figure 4.16

program — program C. After this is done our happy little keyboard junkie looks at Figure 4.14 and panics because there are now no unused blocks on the disk. Deciding that he did not like program B much anyway, he orders its deletion, and is now able to add some extras to program C, which adds one block to its size. Figure 4.15 shows that there are now six free blocks on the disk, but they are fairly well scattered, and even on this minuscule disk this is not a good thing. Before the men from the home drag our demented user away to their white van, he just has time to create another little masterpiece, program D, which occupies four blocks. Had he been able to look at Figure 4.14 he would have seen that we now have three files on the disk, none of which is contiguous, and that the longer the addition and deletion of files goes on the more fragmented will the files become, progressively reducing the speed of retrieval. This is especially true in cases like our example, where disk space is only just sufficient for the job. Sophisticated disk systems can help to some extent, but cannot fully make up for an inefficient file structure.

To illustrate directory fragmentation we will return to the RSTS directories examined earlier in this chapter. Directory fragmentation comes about, like file fragmentation, due to the random nature of users' creation, deletion, and extension of their files. As we saw in the RSTS directory section each file held on the system has a name blockette in a directory. Each name blockette contains a link to the name blockette for the next file. This continues all the way down this "linked list" of entries until a link of zero indicates that the end of the list has been reached. In a similar fashion to that described for files, the directory blockettes are allocated and de-allocated when the files they describe are created and deleted. When users have created many files, the directory will have expanded to take up several clusters (see below). If the directory has never been tidied up, by use of some utility prgram for this purpose, the links can get into a state where the links between the various types of blockettes cross and recross cluster boundaries. This will mean that any time a particular entry in the UFD must be found the directory clusters must be reloaded into memory time and again, ignoring for now the possibility that directory cacheing may be in use. Directory and other cacheing will be examined in chapter six, section B. A simplified representation of a fragmented RSTS UFD is shown in Figure 4.17.

The diagram shows only the name blockettes, and the number of name blockettes – twelve – is of course also the number of files. The diagram shows the search path which must be followed in this appallingly fragmented directory in order to access the name blockette (NB) for the file "MYFILE". Each time the search path crosses the cluster boundaries a fresh cluster will have to be loaded, with repeated loading of the same clusters. The exact figures for this search are:

First cluster is loaded three times (including first access).
Second cluster is loaded four times.
Third cluster is loaded three times.
Total is ten disk accesses (ten cluster loads).

The total number of disk accesses is to find the file's name blockette only. When, as in most cases, its retrieval information, accounting information and possibly attributes information must be found as well, the number of disk accesses can be phenomenal. This "worst case" example illustrates the value of directory maintenance. Programs for performing RSTS directory maintenance (e.g. the RSTS "REORDER" program) try to reorganise the directories in such a way that all the name blockettes are in adjacent blocks in a cluster. This will minimise or eliminate this cross referencing between clusters. It is a good idea to perform this kind of directory maintenance even if directory cacheing is in use, since even though cacheing can sometimes eliminate disk I/O in directory searches this is not always the case.

Start here

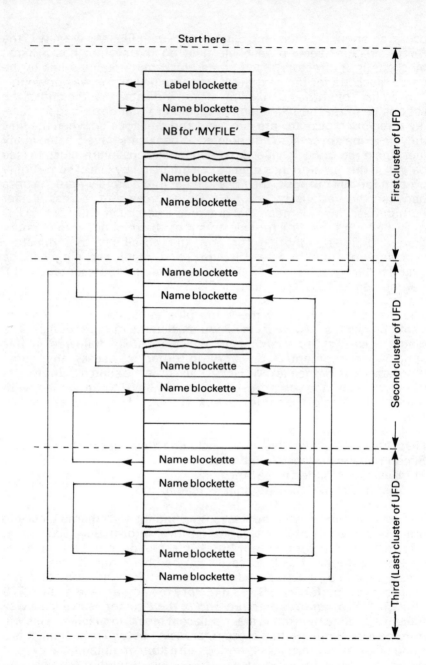

Figure 4.17   RSTS UFD with badly fragmented structure

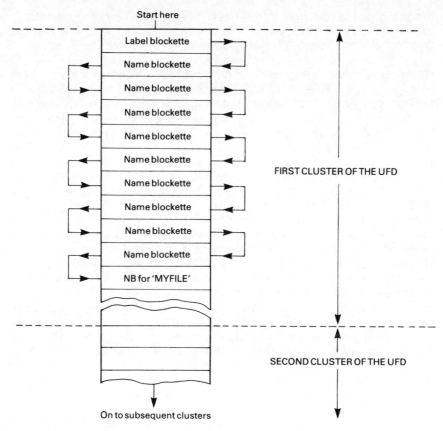

Start here

Label blockette

Name blockette

Name blockette

Name blockette

Name blockette

Name blockette

Name blockette

Name blockette

Name blockette

Name blockette

NB for 'MYFILE'

FIRST CLUSTER OF THE UFD

SECOND CLUSTER OF THE UFD

On to subsequent clusters

Figure 4.18   RSTS UFD after directory maintenance performed

Figure 4.18 shows our simplified directory after being cleaned up in the manner described. There is now no need for any other than the first cluster to be accessed in finding the name blockette for the required file. Thus the directory reordering has resulted in reducing to one-tenth the disk I/O required for the location of the name blockette for this particular file.

More generally, the exact method used to improve the efficiency of a file structure depends upon what software is available to do the job. The most important thing to discover is whether the files, the directories or both are fragmented. The best advice on any particular system will be available from specialist software maintenance staff, but here are some general guidelines on the subject which hold good for many systems.

Fragmented directories are best dealt with by the directory maintenance programs which are usually supplied with the system. Dealing with file fragmentation is often a more complex business.

Utilities are sometimes provided with systems to optimise the disk file storage (e.g. the RSX and VMS systems use "DSC" — "Disc Save and Compress" — which can make files contiguous and place them on disk in optimum positions to achieve fast loading and access, also achieving maximum contiguity of the free blocks on the disk). Where this type of utility is not provided the system manager will probably be advised by software maintenance staff to use some kind of file transfer program to copy all his files from his fragmented disk mounted on another disk drive unit, specifying that the files created on the new disk be made contiguous. At the end of such an operation (which can be very time consuming) the newly created disk will be run instead of the fragmented disk. This will almost certainly result in a noticeable and manifest improvement if the old disk was very badly fragmented. The process will have to be done again, however, when the new disk has been in use for a while and the speed improvement wears off as the new disk begins to get fragmented. Systems which have been in use for some time, yet have never had any file structure maintenance performed on their disks, will very likely be running at far below their capabilities. Becuse of the extra work needed to run a badly maintained file structure the disk units are under two kinds of pressure. First, the system may well become "disk bound" (see glossary), because of the fact that the disks are tied up for longer by purely "system" work, as opposed to user work. Users already accessing files will be impeded, since they may have to wait for lengthy directory searches to be completed. The second pressure is a purely hardware one: that the amount of disk head movement will be greatly increased which, if the problem is severe enough, can result in shortened life of mechanical parts like bearings and motors. This problem of the hardware being made to work unnecessarily hard by software is often called "thrashing". The term is also applied to excessive user swapping (see chapter six).

4.4 Clusters

Grouping disk blocks into clusters (or buckets, as they are sometimes called) can be a good thing, ensuring that disk files are more contiguous, and that consequently they load more quickly and with less CPU involvement in the process. There are, however, some drawbacks under certain conditions in making the cluster size too large.

In the case there are a large number of small files on disk, and here I intend the term small files to apply to files which are smaller than the disk cluster size. Then the cluster size should be as small as possible — or, if the system allows, do not use the concept of file clusters at all. This case, of a great percentage of files being very small, is going to be rare — perhaps only found in schools or colleges or similar educational or training systems. Operating systems like Berkeley UNIX enforce a cluster size of two blocks per cluster, but generally cluster sizes are changeable within the range 2 – 16 blocks per cluster.

Another consideration to apply to deciding what the minimum cluster size is going to be is the amount of disk storage space you have on a specific machine. If, when a system or new disk subsystem is purchased, the buyer has enough foresight — or cash — to buy disk units with enough storage capacity to ensure that there will be at least 25 per cent of the disk blocks unused once all the data and software is installed on the disks, then there is good justification for going for the maximum allowable cluster size. But if, due to lack of money or foresight, the disk storage space purchased is only just enough for the job — leaving less than 25 per cent free, then the cluster size should probably be around half the maximum allowable, or even the minimum if, as previously explained, there are many small files on the system. The reason for these problems is that, when files are created, the system will always allocate disk space in chunks of one cluster, even if the file to be stored in them does not require all the blocks in the cluster. The residue are in effect wasted, except insofar as they are available should extension of the file ever be required.

As an example of this wastage factor consider the three files shown stored in a 16-block cluster in Figure 4.19. The three files are three, fourteen and nine blocks long respectively. This means that, of the 48 blocks allocated for the three clusters, only 26 are used — just over half. Where the average size of the files is larger than a cluster, the wastage factor will drop considerably, since at least one cluster will have 100 per cent usage. If we reduce the cluster size to four, then of the eight clusters now required for the storage of the files, only six out of a total of 32 blocks are wasted. This arrangement is far less wasteful. See Figure 4.20.

One further point about large cluster sizes: where a whole cluster must be read into memory, 8Kb of memory will be required to act as a buffer. If the size of the cluster is large, for example 16 blocks. This will be a large drain on the system buffer pool, and when the buffer pool is small it may have a very bad effect upon system performance. If the whole cluster is not read into memory all at once, the extra benefit gained by the cluster concept may be lost.

77

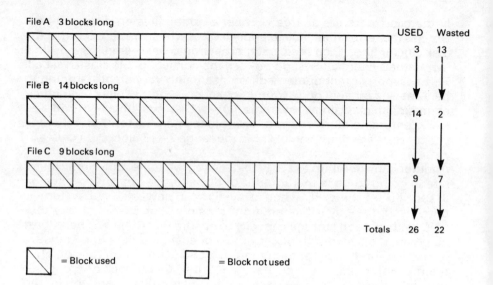

File A   3 blocks long

USED   Wasted

3   13

File B   14 blocks long

14   2

File C   9 blocks long

9   7

Totals   26   22

= Block used   = Block not used

Figure 4.19   Three files of 3, 14, 9 blocks in length respectively stored within three clusters 16 blocks in length.

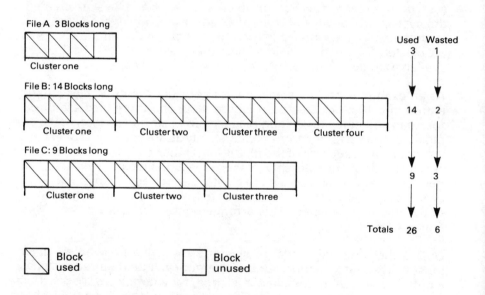

File A   3 Blocks long

Cluster one

Used   Wasted

3   1

File B: 14 Blocks long

Cluster one   Cluster two   Cluster three   Cluster four

14   2

File C: 9 Blocks long

Cluster one   Cluster two   Cluster three

9   3

Totals   26   6

Block used   Block unused

Figure 4.20   Three files of 3, 14 and 9 blocks length respectively, stored within eight clusters of four blocks length.

To sum up, the use of clustering is a good way to slow down the fragmentation of files. It results in increased loading speeds of disk files, and reduced CPU time being expended on disk accesses.

I have here presented some of the concepts of file structuring, its benefits and its pitfalls. The general subject of file structures is a very complex one, and an exhaustive study would fill many volumes – and has – but readers are advised to dig deeper into a file structure with which they have experience as users. I have used the RSTS file structure in my example for this reason. If possible, take a binary, octal, or HEX dump of your directory, and see what you can make of it, but have some aspirin handy.

CHAPTER 5
The Error of Our Ways

5.1 Error Logging – How It Functions

Any salesman who uses 100 per cent reliability as a sales pitch for a computer will try to sell some great national edifice as well, if his potential customer seems to believe his claims. Computers are very complex, and accordingly can be guaranteed to malfunction at some point. It would be true to say that some designs are more failure-prone than others, but usage and environment play a part as well. More important in practical terms than chasing 100 per cent reliability is information about any faults or failures within the machine. If comprehensive information about these is available, diagnosis and fixing can be very much facilitated. Most modern operating systems feature – either as standard or as an optional extra – some form of error logging.

So how does error logging function? The usual pattern is for components of the operating system which detect errors to send all the relevant information describing the error to the error logger, normally in a message format. The error logger itself can be a module of the operating system or a user level program. The messages which are received by the error logger are often sent via a standard mechanism, used by the normal jobs or processes to send one another messages. Upon receiving the details of an error, the error logger must save to a special disk file, all the relevant details in some format for later retrieval by a user level error display program. This user level display program will format the information into easily understandable form, and usually annotate the meaning of device registers, and provide details about date, time, etc. When the information is printed out the system programmers and/or maintenance engineers can scratch their heads over it and hopefully come to a fast conclusion about what needs to be repaired or replaced. Error logging does have a few dangers under some circumstances.

Consider the case where a disk error has occurred. The details are passed to the error logger, which begins to initiate the writing of information into the error log file. If the disk unit is only part-functional as a result of some internal fault having just occurred, the disk I/O occasioned by writing to the error log could easily cause a fresh disk error. A vicious circle has now been entered. Assuming that the disk does not fail altogether, the error log could now grow and grow, due to each fresh entry generating more and more errors which the logger tries to log. If the error log file is not limited in size, the eventual outcome could be that the log file takes up all the spare space on the disk! Thankfully, the maximum size of the error log file is usually fixed. This limitation makes it very important that the error log file be cleared out regularly, after the contents have been printed off or at least examined. If the error log file is full of "junk" or very old entries, it may lead to a serious error going unrecorded, making the cause far more difficult to trace.

Generally the error logging on any system is one of the greatest aids to a fast and accurate diagnosis and fixing of system faults. Diagnostic programs will perform the same function, but will often not trap faults which show up only under the operating system. If system managers are aware of the correct usage and procedures involved in running an error logging system, they can expect to derive a good deal of benefit.

Having this great aid to hardware maintenance at our disposal, we now have to decide what constitutes an error. For example, do we count a device being off line as an error? We might if the device was previously on line and working. If, on the other hand, a user attempted to use a device before ensuring that it was on line, we would probably not. The question of defining errors can also be taken on another level. As discussed in chapter two, section B, a decision had to be taken at design time. If an operation on, say a disk unit, fails, it will normally be retried. Should an entry be made in the error log for each retry? Or should just one entry be made in the event that all retries are unsuccessful? In addition to the error log, error counters are kept on many systems. These are simply memory locations reserved for use as counters. On detection of an error on a specific device its error counter is incremented by one. In such an arrangement, if the maximum count is reached the count goes back to zero. These error counts are useful to engineers where some system failure has caused the error logger to fail, as he can still see how many errors have been logged on the individual hardware units of the system. Under RSTS the "SYS/DF" command will normally show these counters. Under VMS the DCL "SHOW ERROR" command will show peripheral, CPU and memory error counts, likewise for RSX systems using DCL. The counters also provide valuable information where, due to bad management or bad luck, the error log file is full of irrelevant information. As well as errors, many error logging schemes use the logging mechanism to keep track of other system events, like the mounting (see glossary) or dismounting of tapes, disks or other removable media on systm devices. RSX and VMS both write "time stamps" as well. These are especially useful where the system is crashing and not restarting itself. (In section C of this chapter we shall look at the subject of system crashes and crash dumps). Other entries in the error log may be system startups and shutdowns, and other events like printers running out of paper etc.

Error logs are produced to aid software and hardware engineers, and make their lives a lot easier. It is always possible that they can also confuse, if sufficient experience or intelligence is not applied to the provided information. For example: if an error is logged for every retry performed, the first entry might be the only real error. However, due to this error having caused the device to drop its online and ready status, there will be a number of follow-on entries in the error log. Follow-on entries occur because many devices – especially disks – drop their online and ready status immediately their internal fault detection electronics detect some types of error. If the software begins an operation which at first try brings on such a fault, all the retries will fail simply because the device is offline. The error log entries will therefore show one real error and a number of knock-on entries (the exact number being dependent on how many retries the device driver attempts), which merely state that the device is offline. This forcing offline feature found on many devices is to protect not only data, but also, media, and on some devices (like disks) the unit itself. It is easy for an inexperienced person to look through an error log containing one real error and conclude that the device dropping offline was the cause of the whole problem. Once again, if the error log is filled with old entries there will arise a far greater diffculty in diagnosing a transitory fault if the initial error as cited above occurs.

So much for the concepts, benefits and pitfalls of error logging. Now we will examine some system-specific examples of error logs, extracted from actual error logs produced by RSTS, RSX and VMS.

5.2 Error Log Examples

Example 1   RSTS: "CK RTS DECLARED".

When a user causes a BASIC-PLUS program to be saved to disk in compiled form (compiled here means a machine-coded program implementing a program written in BASIC-PLUS source statements). The BASIC-PLUS language (or RUN TIME) system writes — within the data block — a checksum of all the contents. This is the only class of file for which this occurs, as if a source program were loaded badly the BASIC-PLUS compiler would not recognise some part of the source statements and would not run the program. However, in the case of a compiled program, the file containing the program is loaded and run, with no further compilation being needed. This has the implication that if there were some corruption of the code being loaded which either occurred during the transfer between the disk controller and memory, or which somehow slipped by the data verification mechanisms within the disk controller, then the corrupted code might crash the system. This corruption need only lead to making an alteration in the RSTS area of memory, or somehow disabling clock interrupts, and the whole system could go out of control or get stuck in a loop. These, then, are the reasons for adding this additional data verification method for compiled BASIC-PLUS programs.

In the case of a badly-loaded compiled program, the BASIC-PLUS run time system (RTS) declares to the error logging program "ERRCPY" a checksum error, because the incoming checksum from disk does not match the one it has just calculated of the loaded data. A printout of the entry which is created in the error log for such an event is shown in Figure 5.1.

This class of error occurs as a result of a DMA failure or memory error which goes undetected. It can occur at either the time a compiled BASIC file is written, or at the time it is read. When it occurs during the writing stage what happens is that the disk controller writes into the file the information it receives from memory as a result of a DMA read, but is unable to detect that the information it has received is not the same as was originally contained in the memory. This can be due to bit changes in faulty memory which have occurred since the information was placed there, or because the information was corrupted somewhere in its journey across the bus from memory to the disk controller. When a failure occurs at the read stage a similar thing happens. The memory into which the controller places the data

```
ERRDIS Full Report (CK only) taken on 09-Nov-83, 21:14
Input File: (1,2)ERRLOG.FIL      Output File: LP:

Requested Date/Time Range:
        First Error through Last Error

(1,2)ERRLOG.FIL will not be Zeroed upon completion


**********************************************************************
CK   RTS Declared Seq £3 Occurred on 09-Nov-83 at 21:14:01

User Description:
------------------
Job Number                5
KB Number                 0
Account                   [1,19]
Program Name              SYSTAT
User Job Physical Addr.    00600000
User Job Size             12K
Control Parameters        200
RTS Name                  BASIC
RTS Physical Address      00210000

Detailed Description:
---------------------
R0                        000000
R1                        001126
R2                        120454
R3                        106671
R4                        000402
R5                        112364
Virtual PC                147310
Physical PC               00257310
Processor Status          170000
Stack Pointer             000374
(SP)                      000000
(SP+2)                    000000
(PC-6)                    020503
(PC-4)                    001405
(PC-2)                    104052
(PC)                      005067
CPU ID                    0
CPU ERR                   000000
```

Figure 5.1

84

fails to retain it, or the information output across the bus by the disk controller is altered by some hardware problem. In either case the disk controller cannot detect an error because it has written what it received, or read exactly what was written, or sent the correct data to memory. So this type of error is not really a disk failure, but rather a system failure. The cause of the error can usually be ascertained by analysis of the entry in the error log. The entry in the error log shows the following items of information (see Figure 5.1):

The job number.

The user's keyboard number.

The address in memory at which the user job was residing (physical address).

The contents of the CPU registers.

The contents of the address pointed to by the stack pointer register, and some of the addresses around it.

The name of the program which was being loaded.

The time and date of the error.

The error which the printout describes was deliberately induced on an PDP-11/34a system. The job number was five. The keyboard was kbO: (the keyboard console). The account was 1,19 . The address values, register contents and memory contents shown are all in Octal.

Looking at the "user job size" entry, the size shown is 12KW. By reference to a directory listing we can find the size of the file containing the program. In the directory this will be expressed as the number of blocks. Given that there are 512 bytes per block we can get the amount of memory which the full files would occupy by dividing the number of blocks by four (since four times 512 bytes is equal to 1KW). Referring to the "user job size" in the sample printout we can see that the size at the time of the error was 12KW. "SYSTAT" usually occupies 13KW (see Figure 7.6, showing the output of "SYSTAT" in which it shows the job sizes). BEWARE: this simplistic approach ignores size distortions which may be introduced by minimum cluster sizes. If a second attempt at running the file produces an entry in the error log which shows identical results, then the file was badly written. If it loads without any problem, the error was almost certainly the result of a bus problem during the failed load. This class of error occurs fairly frequently on RSTS systems, and unfortunately is often misinterpreted as a conventional disk error, which it is not.

Example 2   VMS ECC Memory Error

The VAX processors, on which VMS runs, feature Error Correction Code – ECC – on their memory subsystems. With ECC installed memory errors such as the spurious dropping or raising of single bits in memory can be detected and corrected. In this way memory which on non-ECC machines would be unusable remains operable, because the ECC can calculate the correct state of the bit which has changed. Single bit errors are logged by the VMS error logger as shown in Figure 5.2a. It should be borne in mind here that this report was of an error which, although running an unmodified version of DEC VMS, did not have DEC memory. This is important here because the DEC memory (at the time of writing) is organised as 256K of memory per memory board, whereas the machine this log was taken from had some other manufacturer's memory boards installed which contained one megabyte of memory per board. Due to this some of the values shown are not as they would be for a 100 per cent DEC machine. However, the information provided is still sufficient to locate the failing bit on the failing chip, on the failing board when taken in conjunction with memory board chip layouts and diagrams.

In the report shown the memory base address is zero. Thus we know that the board acting as the lowest megabyte of memory contains the faulty circuitry. We can see that the failing bit is 21 (remember that the 1MB is actually used as 32 bit memory by the VAX processor). The error syndrome is the information which is produced by the ECC to identify the failing bit. The CSRO – CSR2 entries shown are the contents of the three Control Status Registers for the memory. Additionally the error log contains the exact time and date of the error and the SID (System Identification number – each processor has its own number). The memory controller type is shown, as is the size of the failing board (1024K = 1M). This report could, and indeed did, point the hardware engineer straight to the problem area, allowing the faulty board to be replaced before irreversible errors began occurring.

The VMS error reporting is first class, and at the end of every standard format error report the VMS error log printout program SYE prints a histogram of all the errors it has logged; this is very valuable where some kind of error occurs at a set time (perhaps as a result of mains fluctuation caused by some timer-controlled machine connected to the same circuit elsewhere in a building). This histogram is shown in Figure 5.2b.

```
*************************** ENTRY    03. ***************************
ERROR SEQUENCE 1363.                          LOGGED ON SID 020051F1

MEMORY ERROR, 19-OCT-1983 08:15:10.43 KA750 REVE 255. MICE 94.

CONTROLLER AT SLOT INDEX EO.

        CSR0            20134975
                                    ERROR SYNDROME = 75
                                    CORRECTED ERROR, BIT E21.
                                    ARRAY E420. IN ERROR
                                    CORRECTED ERROR FLAG
        CSR1            10000000
                                    ENABLE REPORTING CORRECTED ERRORS
        CSR2            6E0000FF
                                    MEMORY SIZE = 1024.K
                                    MEMORY BASE ADDRESS = O.K
                                    CONTROLLER IS L0011
                                            LOGGED ON SID 020051F1
```

Figure 5.2a

```
V A X / V M S        SYSTEM ERROR REPORT        COMPILED 19-OCT-1983 09:35
                                                            PAGE  38.


SUMMARY OF ALL ENTRIES LOGGED BY SID 020051F1

            MEMORY ERROR                      6.
            ERRLOG.SYS CREATED                1.
            TIME-STAMP                       24.

            DATE OF EARLIEST ENTRY       12-OCT-1983 12:16:24.73
            DATE OF LATEST ENTRY         19-OCT-1983 09:26:24.74

PROCESSED ENTRIES HOUR-OF-DAY HISTOGRAM LOGGED BY SID 020051F1

            00:00      15. ***************
            01:00       0.
            02:00       0.
            03:00       0.
            04:00       0.
            05:00       0.
            06:00       0.
            07:00       0.
            08:00       4. ****
            09:00      14. **************
            10:00       0.
            11:00       2. **
            12:00       1. *
            13:00       2. **
            14:00       0.
            15:00       0.
            16:00       6. ******
            17:00       7. *******
            18:00       0.
            19:00       0.
            20:00       0.
            21:00       8. ********
            22:00       8. ********
            23:00      10. **********
```

Figure 5.2b

88

Example 3   RSX TT error.

TT (user terminal) errors occur fairly frequently on many systems, not only RSX. They can be due to an error bit set in the UART or USART set in the terminal interface at the time the system was accessing it, or they can be due to the processor having missed a character due to not responding quickly enough to an interrupt from the interface. In general these errors are not particularly serious, since output to terminals is usually fairly ephemeral, and if it comes up with characters missing, it may not be noticed, or the user at the terminal will request the same information again. Where the terminal errors might be serious is if a printer is connected to a serial terminal line – as often happens with dot matrix printers or letter-quality printers. If for some reason the output here is scrambled and goes unnoticed, the problem might become more acute. The most serious terminal errors will be when errors occur when inputting data to the system. Where these occur in great numbers, some item of hardware must be malfunctioning and will have to be fixed. When an error is logged on an RSX system, the interface or controller register contents are shown and, using them in conjunction with the relevant hardware manuals, the error can be specified and tackled.

5.3 Analysing system crashes and determining their causes.

A computer can suffer one or two catastrophic error conditions. First, it can hang up. A "system hang" is where the machine still echoes things typed into it from terminals, but does not respond to commands typed in, or in some cases does not respond properly to them. When a "system crash" has occurred the system will not echo or respond to anything typed into it, at any terminal.

The two terms "system hang" and "system crash" are often confused, but although they may both be caused by similar faults in different degrees it is extremely important to differentiate between them.
An operating system may "hang up" for a great many reasons. We shall now list a few.

1) The body of machine code resident in memory which comprises the operating system becomes corrupted. This can be due to faulty memory, or accidental or malicious alteration of some vital part by user programs or external events such as power dips. The net results of a corrupted operating system are likely to be execution of incorrect

jump or branch instructions, or bad program flow caused by bad semaphores or flags. When this happens certain parts of the operating system may become traps into which any user attempting to use them will fail. This is sometimes a cause of "user hang" (see reason 4 below).

2) Some previously undiscovered bug in the operating system comes to light. Given the millions of possible pathways through a multi user system this may occur in the early days of use of any operating system. The result may be a cessation of orderly execution of operating system code, with unpredictable results ensuing, nonsensical error messages, etc.

3) Another common cause of "system hang" is a failure in, or incorrect connection to, one or more terminal interfaces. If a terminal interface fails in such a way as to permanently assert an interrupt request, or if a disconnected terminal line picks up random noise and sends in a continuous stream of spurious characters as a result, the system may appear to hang up. Terminal lines with their send and receive lines shorted together are the worst offenders here.

4) A related problem to "system hang" is "user hang" (or "job hang"). "User hang" is not what some system managers would like to do to their more troublesome users, but rather describes the condition where just one user's job or terminal response freezes. Usually the other users on the system are unaffected and run normally. This can be due to a number of things. For example, some versions of RSTS will appear to hang up a job after the user has commanded a search of a magnetic tape for a particular file, using the PIP file transfer utility. The user may try to abort the search and return to command level, by typing the CRTL/C combination, but the only conditions under which this will happen are the file being found, the EOT character being encountered or an error on the tape unit occurring (for example, the exasperated user taking the tape unit offline). If the tape is long, the search may last for many minutes, and the user's job will appear to be hung. Other reasons for "user hang" are where the user is waiting for service from an operating system component which it never recieves (e.g. the file processor); or when a device allocated to the user's exclusive use malfunctions, never completing an operation, or corruption of system information relating to the hung job.

"System hang" should be investigated carefully, since if the system can be freed up, this will be better than crashing the system by force by halting and restarting. If the cause is not firmly established the likelihood of a repeat of the problem is high. Commonly engineers will attempt to cure a "system hang" by trying to log into the system at a higher priority than any other user, and then halt or remove other users from the system one by one until normal operation is resumed. Unplugging each terminal line in turn is another method. Another is to use some system monitor program, which may show which device is hogging the system, and if possible disable it. All these methods imply some minimal functionality of the system, which in many cases is not available. If it is not possible to free the system up by these means, the only recourse is to halt and reboot the system.

Finding the cause of a system crash can be extremely easy or really difficult. The deciding factor is often the availability or absence of a crash dump. When an operating system is informed by external fault detect mechanisms (e.g. power supply fail, or a memory fault within the area occupied by the operating system, etc.) then, for reasons of user protection and security, the operating system will deem a so-called catastrophic event to have taken place. Under such conditions the system will write the contents of the processor, the memory and any other relevant information about the system at the time of the crash into a crash dump file. The operating system will then reload itself and restart from scratch. During the restart the new copy of the operating system will typically detect that the disks of the system were not left in the proper state and will do a disk check on the directory integrity, and either fix any discrepancies found or ask the system manager if the fixing is required. During such crashes there may be some information lost, though to a large extent this will depend on the way in which the user level programs are written, and specifically whether any disk I/O was taking place at the exact instant of the crash. The contents of the crash dump file will be formatted and annotated into a printout for analysis by hardware and software staff. The main thing to look for in a crash dump is the crash code or error code. This will indicate what the operating system was informed of, or detected, which made it write the crash dump and restart. This code is usually a pretty good indicator, but if the fault detection circuitry itself is faulty, then it can be worthless.

The more difficult type of crash is the "total" or "halt" type. If the operating system falls victim to a sudden hardware fault (e.g. one of the data or address bus lines suddenly being held high or low by some interface or controller developing a fault), then the processor may go into "runaway" – executing a random instruction sequence ending up by executing instructions at any part of memory until a halt instruction is executed. (This is one reason that unused memory on most computers is filled with the code for "halt".) Probably the most important (though, because of the "runaway" problem, not to be taken as an absolute indicator) item is the contents of the program counter at the time that the system halted, or halted itself. If the system can be restarted then another good thing to do is to search the error log for recent errors which may show that some item of the computer (rather than its peripherals) has been troublesome. It could be, in such a case, that the troublesome item of hardware has worsened and caused the crash. If the system can be restarted, and the contents of the program counter were obtained, then look at a map of the operating system's internal layout and see which component of it occupies the memory area which most closely corresponds to the PC value. If the system cannot be restarted, then of course it comes down to fault-finding each item of hardware present within the computer and its peripherals until a restart becomes possible. In many cases — certainly in the case of our sample systems — the crash dump is an option, so that it must be enabled to be automatic; otherwise the system will restart itself without writing a dump into the crash file.

As a very unsophisticated rule of thumb, the "total" crash which always yields the same PC contents can be due to an operating system bug, or in extreme cases a bug in a user level program which for some reason the operating system or a language interpreter is not able to protect against. Crashes which are more random in nature are more likely to be due to hardware problems. Neither of these generalisations should be taken as a regular rule, but rather as a rough and ready guideline.

Analysing and interpreting crash dumps is a very specialised business, requiring access to piles of tomes on the operating system concerned, and a great deal of knowledge and experience in the field. The system utility program which formats and annotates the crash dump can, however, often give a perfectly accurate assessment of the cause which will prevent the need for the involvement of such a specialist, who will be consulted only in those cases where the causes and effects seem contradictory or just obscure.

When RSTS writes a crash dump, it writes the dump into a file called "CRASH.SYS" which should exist in the account 0,1 . The dump is written when RSTS gets a power fail signal or detects a memory parity fault in the area of memory in which it is resident, or some other condition from which it cannot recover. Once the dump is written a full restart is executed if possible. Once the system is back up, the "ANALYS" program should be run. This takes the contents of the dump file and prints it out to the file or device specified by you. A useful feature is that the dump can be annotated by appending "/ WIDE" to the output device or file name (e.g. "LP:/WIDE"). This will make "ANALYS" provide annotations to the memory contents, which may at least prove interesting, and might even be of assistance. Once the dump has been printed the error code may indicate the fault. If not, then look through the contents of the CPU registers (RO – R5) and see if any of their contents look like interface or controller addresses. Another important thing to look at in a RSTS crash dump is the current job number: i.e. the number of the user who was currently having his runburst of CPU time at the instant of the crash. Match the job number (in Octal, remember) to the list of jobs at the top of the dump, and look under the "WHAT" column for this job. If the program which was running was a new unproven one (especially a transplanted program which was compiled on a different system) then look at the possibility of this causing the crash – either by running it again or by consulting with its writer or a software expert. Incidentally, if the crash caused by a memory failure and there is a job shown whose "WHAT" column is empty, then the system may well have crashed whist trying to access some previously unused memory to allocate to a user just logging into the system.

Now refer to Figures 5.4a through to 5.4e. These are the first five pages of the printout from a RSTS crash dump. Applying what has been said above, we can see that there were 14 jobs on the system. The error code was for a power fail; this could mean that the power supplies had detected a fail in the incoming mains voltage, or that the actual output voltage from one of the power supply modules was falling below a preset level. In either case only a small time is available before the voltages of the supply fall below a level at which the processor will "die". This short time is used to do the crash dump. Another interesting thing in the dump is the job number being processed at the time of the crash. In this case both the current and the next job number is zero. This implies that RSTS was itself running and had not scheduled another job for a runburst (perhaps because there was no point, since the power supply was almost gone). The saved CPU registers RO – R5 are all zeroes except RO, R1 and R3. RO contains an I/O address, which in this case is a base address of the disk controller for this particular system. It would be reasonable to assume that the disk controller was being loaded at the time that the CPU registers contained these values, and if there were not a definite indication in the error code of a power fail then the disk controller might be eligible for a thorough examination. This crash would not seem to have been a very dangerous one, since if we look down the crash dump status we can see that at the time of the crash almost all the users were idling (as indicated by uparrow C in their respective "State" columns), or sleeping (shown by "SL" or "SR") or waiting for keyboard input ("KB" in state column). The only job in actual run (RN) mode was the progrm which copies details of errors detected on the system into the error data file. This program "ERRCPY" is not only running, but if you look at its priority level (under the PRI/RB heading) you will see that all other jobs were running at − 8, whilst the "ERRCPY" was running at 0 priority − which is higher. This is in order that a job with a higher priority cannot generate errors faster than "ERRCPY" can write details of them into the error data file. (The log-in default priority for a RSTS user job is is − 8, although privileged users can alter their priority and their runburst length). The list of files open on the system enables the system manager to know where to look for file corruptions. This will typically only happen where a crash occurs during a file or directory update, or when a pointer chain within a data file is broken. The crash analysis is usually the job of software support staff, and, as has already been stated, is a very specialist job. However, if the points here presented can be appreciated, a crash dump can aid other people as well.

```
Analysis of (0,1)CRASH.SYS/SIL:SY0:(0,1)RSTS.SIL
         Taken on 27-Sep-83 at 16:32

ANALYS run from system: RSTS V7.1-11 RSTS SYSTEM
The system SIL was used.


The following symbols could not be found:
FMSBUF
ANALYS will continue.

System was configured for DECnet/E
System was configured for large files
Configuration word (X.CON) = 004000
Memory segments that were dumped:
        Monitor
        FIP Pool
        XBUF
No 22-bit hardware addressing
CPU hardware did not have I and D space
Monitor did not use I and D space

SATBUF is valid for this dump.
```

FIGS 5.4

```
Crash Dump Status From 23-Aug-83 at 16:55   ,  Up: 7:48:50


Job    Who      Where   What      Size    State    Run-Time   Pri/Rb   RTS
1      1,2      Det     ERRCPY    5/31K   RN C22    10.7       0/6      EASIC
2      1,2      Det     W110PN    4/31K   SL C21    16.2       -8/6     EASIC
3      1,2      Det     QUMRUN    16/31K  SL C19    7.5        0/6      BASIC
4      1,2      Det     OPSRUN    16/31K  SL        35.6       -8/6     BASIC
5      1,2      Det     SPLIDL    16/31K  SL C17    4.7        -8/6     EASIC
6      25,115   KB15    NONAME    2/31K   ^C C09    36.1       -8/6     BASIC
7      1,2      Det     BATIDL    13/31K  SL C18    4.4        -8/6     BASIC
8 -    25,102   KB7     WPSMEN    16/31K  KB        1:00.2     -8/6     BASIC
9      1,25     Det     WPSQUE    16/31K  SR C16    15.5       -8/6     BASIC
10 -   25,118   KB2     WPSMEN    16/31K  K3 C10    4:52.2     -8/6     BASIC
13     1,10     KB0     DCL       2/31K   ^C C12    3.6        -8/6     DCL
14     1,14     KB10    DTR       31/31K  K3 C08    1:12.5     -8/6     ...RSX
15 -   25,115   KB11    WPSMEN    16/31K  KB C14    2:09.0     -8/6     BASIC
16 +   25,60    KB3     WPSEDT    6/31K   KB C13    10:34.9    -8/6     WPSEDT


Busy Devices:
Device   Job      Why
KB18     J*2=1
KB19     J*2=1
KB20     J*2=1
KB21     J*2=1
KB22     J*2=1
KB23     J*2=1
KB24     J*2=1
KB25     J*2=1
KB26     J*2=1


Disk Structure:
Dsk  Open    Size      Free   Clu   Err   Name    Comments
DR0   36    64000     7740   12%    4     0    W11SYS  Pub, DLW
DR1   5     64000     17440  27%    8     0    W11DAT  Pri, NFF, DLW


Open Files:

DR1:%WH -- File              Op/RR   Size   Clu    FRE              NE            Status
[ 1,14 ]CIS    .DIC<60>      1/0     400    4      001204769360  001204769340   Upd
       Job 14   Block 190    Up

[ 1,14 ]CISCON.DAT<60>       1/0     640    64     001204619540  001204619520   Upd
       Job 14   Block 2      Up

[ 1,14 ]CISMAS.DAT<60>       1/0     896    128    001204619200  001204619100   Upd
       Job 14   Block 82     Up

[ 1,1 ]QUERY  .MSG<40>       1/0     478    4      000000119060  000000109560
       Job 14   Block 34

[ 1,14 ]TEMP16.TMP< 0>       1/0     20     4      001204629540  001204629060   MDL
       Job 14   Block 2

[ 1,2 ]DTR    .TSK<104>      0/1     371    4      000764139000  000764119700   Ctg
       Job 14   Block 111    RR

[ 1,25 ]WPSEDT.WPS<252>      0/1     9      4      001061629500  001061629460
       Job 16   Block 1      RR

[ 0,1 ]DCL    .DCL<232>      0/1     1      4      000001629320  000001629300   Pla, Ctg
       Job 13   Block 0      RR

[ 1,25 ]WORD11.WPS<252>      1/0     3      8      777777779775  001061619740
```


Figure 5.4b

```
            Job 2    Block 0

[ 1,25 ]WPSTSK.TSK<60>     1/0      6     4   0010617009300 001061709220
            Job 2    Block 0

[ 1,25 ]WPSANA.DAT<60>     1/0     194    32  00106167a260 001061629040  Ctg
            Job 2    Block 0

[ 1,25 ]WPSMEN.BAC<232>    1/0     59     4   00106161a520 001061611460
            Job 2    Block 0

[ 1,25 ]WPSQUE.DAT< 0>     1/0     16     4   00106162a260 001061669720
            Job 9    Block 2

[ 1,2  ]BATC07.WRK< 0>     1/0      9     4   00076415a040 000764169620
            Job 7    Block 1

[ 1,25 ]WPSMEN.WPS<60>     3/0     20     4   00106170a260 001061709240
            Job 8    Block 2
            Job 15   Block 10
            Job 10   Block 2

[ 1,2  ]SPL005.WRK< 0>     1/0      7     4   00076416a560 000764159200
            Job 5    Block 1

[ 1,5  ]QUEUE .WRK<60>     1/0     11     4   00031663a260 000316639240
            Job 3    Block 2

[ 1,2  ]QUEUE .SYS<40>     1/0     24     4   00076416a540 000764159720
            Job 3    Block 1

[ 1,5  ]TEMP03.TMP< 0>     1/0     14     4   00031663a300 000316639200  MDL
            Job 3    Block 19

[ 1,10 ]OPSER .LOG< 0>     1/0      0     4   7777777a776 001062419120
            Job 4    Block 0

[ 1,2  ]OPSER1.WRK<40>     2/0     21     4   00076412a440 00076412a420
            Job 3    Block 0
            Job 4    Block 1

[ 1,5  ]OPSER0.WRK<60>     1/0      2     4   00031663a140 000316639120
            Job 4    Block 1


DR1: -- File               Op/RR   Size   Clu    FRE             NE        Status
[ 25,115]INDEX .WPS< 0>    1/0      9     8   00006241a060 00006241a040
            Job 15   Block 7

[ 25,60 ]WPSP16.TMP< 0>    1/0     39     8   00054172a320 00054172a300
            Job 16   Block 2

[ 25,60 ]TEMP16.TMP<60>    1/0     32     32  00054172a240 000541719460  MDL
            Job 16   Block 24

[ 25,60 ]WPSO58.WPS< 0>    1/0     76     8   000541733000 00054172a740
            Job 16   Block 37

[ 25,60 ]WPS   .TSK< 0>    1/0      7     8   00166353a300 000542239360
            Job 16   Block 0


General   FIP                   Hung
Buffers   Buffers  Jobs/Jobmax  TTY'S   Errors
```

Figure 5.4c

96

```
   392          0         14/22          0            3
```

Run-Time Systems:

Name	Typ	Size	Users	Comments
BASIC	BAC	16(16)K	11	Perm, Addr:34, KBM, CSZ
RSX	TSK	3(28)K	0	Non-Res, KBM
RT11	SAV	4(28)K	0	Non-Res, KBM, CSZ, EMT:255
DCL		12(2)K	1	Non-Res, DF KBM
WPSEDT		22(8)K	1	Temp, Addr:101
WPSSPL		19(12)K	0	Non-Res
WPSLST		19(12)K	0	Non-Res
WPSSRT		12(20)K	0	Non-Res
WPSSED		4(23)K	0	Non-Res
LEXNEW	S11	9(20)K	0	Non-Res, KBM, CSZ, EMT:255
TECO	TEC	8(24)K	0	Non-Res

Resident Libraries:

Name	Prot	Acct	Size	Users	Comments
EDT	< 42>	[0,1]	21K	0	Non-Res, Addr:103

Message Receivers:

Rcvrid	Job	Rib	Obj	Msgs/Max	Links/Max	Access
ERRLOG	1	0	0	1/40	0/0	Prv
QUEMAN	3	0	0	0/60	0/0	Lcl
OPSER	4	0	0	0/30	0/0	Lcl
LPQSPL	5	0	0	0/5	0/0	Prv
BASPL	7	0	0	0/5	0/0	Prv
WPSQUE	9	0	0	0/60	0/0	Prv

STSTBL:

DSTCTL = 070552   JSTCTL = 070364   CHECTL = 070024

Figure 5.4d

97

Octal Dump of Status

Error Code
027776/ 177777 Power fail

Saved R0 to R5
027760/ 176000 000001 000002 000000 000000 000000

Kernel Stack Pointer
027774/ 002104

Virtual Program Counter
027756/ 074332

Processor Status
027754/ 000040

Next 8. items on Kernel SP stack
027752/ 000000 000000 000000 000000 000000 000000 000000 000000

User Stack Pointer
027732/ 000372

Top 8. items on User SP stack
027730/ 106774 173522 101556 020060 000000 000020 000006 000000

User Keyword
027710/ 020060

User FIRQB
027706/ 000000 000020 000006 000000 000000 000000 000000 000000
027666/ 000000 000000 000000 000000 000000 000000 000000 000000

User XRB
027646/ 000200 000000 021204 000002 000000 000000 000000

Registers in I-Space:

		User Addr. Reg.	User Desc. Reg.	Kernel Addr. Reg.	Kernel Desc. Reg.
027532/	APR0	004500	077406	000000	077506
027542/	APR1	004700	077406	000200	077506
027552/	APR2	005100	077406	000400	077406
027562/	APR3	005300	077406	000600	077506
027572/	APR4	002100	077402	001000	057402
027602/	APR5	002300	077402	001330	077402
027612/	APR6	002500	077402	001664	077006
027622/	APR7	002700	077402	007600	077506

Memory Management Registers:
MMR0
027530/ 000017

MMR2
027526/ 121152

	Job	Next
001006\	000	000

	JOBDA	JOBF	IOSTS	JOBWRK	JOBJD2	JOBRTS	CPUTIM	JOBWDB
001010/	000000	100502	067124	000000	067124	000000	067124	000000

FIJOB
001302\ 020

Figure 5.4e

CHAPTER 6
"On My Left, The Software...On My Right, The Hardware"

Many computer people treat system hardware and system software as two totally separate, isolated disciplines. While it can be appreciated that many hardware engineers do not have any interest or motivation to become involved in system software problems – and that, conversely, many software practitioners shy away like frightened horses from soldering irons – the attitude is to be regretted, because there is a definite overlap area which, if entered, gives a very much clearer insight into many computer problems. This area provides much of the subject matter for this chapter.

6.1 Buffering of Information

Without buffering of information in a computer system, transfer of information between the computer and its peripherals would be difficult, and in some cases impossible. If, for example, a terminal had to successfully receive characters at the rate at which most CPUs can send them, it would quite simply be hopelessly outrun. Of course, the CPU could spend time waiting for the terminal (or its interface) to be ready for another character, but this would be a massive waste of CPU time. Another example is where a text file held on disk is to be printed on a matrix printer attached to a terminal line. The printer can print around 120 – 175 characters every second, whilst the disk unit can transfer 512 characters every two or three milliseconds. We shall return to this example shortly. Buffering has a major part to play in making possible easy, CPU efficient, transfers of information between the computer peripherals and the CPU itself, which is almost certain to be faster than any of them. This speed matching utilises areas of memory as buffers. The basic ideas behind buffering were looked at in Chapter Two, but there will now be a more detailed examination of a practical, though non-specific, scheme for terminal input and output buffering.

Each terminal on the system will, in our generalised scheme, have an input buffer, and an output buffer. The input buffer will be used to store the characters typed on the keyboard, and is in effect an assembly area for the commands, or data being typed in character by character, and upon completion of this assembly (signalled by the entry of a delimiting character such as carriage return or new line) the input buffer will contain a command, or some data for passing on to some other operating system component or language system. The terminals attached to the system all have an output buffer each. Into this output buffer will be put everything which is to be sent out to the terminal. This will include output from user level programs, operating system prompts, messages from other users and messages from operating system components. As an aside, line printer devices will usually have an output buffer, but not an input buffer, because they are only one-way devices, and their output buffer will usually be larger than that for a terminal, due to the faster throughput. Going with a terminal's input and output buffers will be flags and condition indicators. These will indicate whether the buffer is full, and therefore locked against any process placing more data in it. There will probably be a counter which represents the number of characters stored in the buffer. Another will signify which terminal the buffer belongs to (especially when buffers are not dedicated, but are available via a buffer pool manager). Another flag will show whether the data held in the buffer is input FROM the terminal or output FOR it.

When the operating system receives a request from a user process for data to be put into the output buffer of a terminal, it must first ensure that the output buffer for the desired terminal is not locked. When there is no space, the requesting process is put into a wait state (or suspended state), and the condition which will wake it up again is the unlocking of the desired output buffer. The system component which will do the unlocking is the terminal driver — when it has made some space in the output buffer. If there was space in the output buffer to begin with, the buffer is filled with the desired data, and the fill and empty operations will go on until all the data has been transferred. Refer to Figure 6.1, and there in flow diagram form a solution is shown

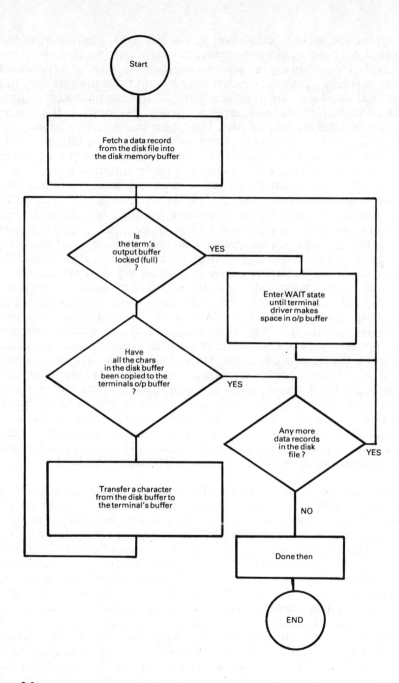

Figure 6.1

to do the job mentioned above, to transfer a text file from disk out to a serial dot matrix printer attached to a terminal line. Returning to the subject of the input buffer, when a character is typed at a terminal the code corresponding to the character is sent from the terminal to the terminal interface. The interface then generates a hardware interrupt. The next step is that the operating system responds to the interrupt by running the terminal driver. The typed character is now evaluated to see if it is a printable character, or whether it is a character which the operating system regards as special. If the character is printable, it is echoed — sent back to the terminal via its output buffer. Unless the character is special (in which case it is usually actioned immediately) it is placed into the terminal's input buffer, unless the input buffer is full. Where the input buffer is discovered to be full some indication must be given to the user that he has typed in too many characters, since the maximum number of characters which a terminal input buffer can accomodate will be longer than the longest valid command sequence. This buffer overflow indication will sometimes take the form of an error message. For example, RSTS gives the error message "LINE TOO LONG". Another indicator can be that the system will echo anything typed in with a bell character, so that whatever is typed the terminal will bleep. The prime example of the special characters mentioned above is a line terminator, like carriage return, or on some systems, the Escape character. These indicate that the whole line has now been entered, and that interpretation of what was typed in can now begin. On detecting a line terminator, the terminal driver will pass either the address of the input buffer or its contents to the parsing routines which will interpret its contents, or if the user is responding to a prompt issued by a user level program the input will be passed to the program. In Chapter Seven, Section Three, we shall examine other hardware devices for character I/O from terminals.

Larger buffers are required for I/O to block transfer devices. The size of these buffers will vary, depending upon the number of block transfer devices attached to a particular hardware configuration, and the amount of overall memory available. The size of the large buffer(s) should be large enough to take at least one block from the device with the biggest transfer size. The dangers of large transfer sizes were outlined in Chapter Four, when "cluster sizes" for disks were discussed. It should be added here that in hardware terms block data transfers can cause many random timing problems, if the hardware is not designed or set up properly. If, for example, there were a disk controller attached to a system bus which transferred data at a higher hardware priority than any other device or controller, then once the disk controller had begun a block transfer, or worse, a multiple block transfer, all other controllers — and of course the CPU — would be locked out for the duration of the transfer. This could easily result in some event like a character typed at a keyboard being lost, due to being overwritten by the next one before it was transferred from the terminal interface to memory by the CPU. In practice this hardly ever happens, though due to peaks of bus demands it cannot be ruled out as a once-in-a-lifetime occurrence. Hardware designers build into block transfer controllers a transfer count (sometimes called a throttle count). This specifies the number of bytes, or words, or longwords which may be transferred between the controller and memory before the bus is relinquished to allow another device to transfer some data across it. After a small "off bus" time the controller will regain the bus, and another few transfers take place. In this way other bus users are only locked out for short periods. The exact number of transfers to be performed by such a controller is usually selected by one of two methods. One: the count is specified by the operating system, by means of writing the number into a special regiser on board the controller. Two: the count is specified by a set of links or pencil (DIL) switches on the controller; this method will enable hardware maintenance staff to optimise a particular configuration's performance. The addition of this few-transfers-at-a-time approach greatly complicates the design of a controller, as some new kind of buffering within the controller will now be needed. In the case of a disk or magnetic tape controller the data comes off the medium in a block and cannot be stalled in mid-block because the controller has lost the use of the bus, thus an internal buffer must be used.

Buffers are used in matching the speed of peripheral devices to the CPU, and also to one another. They are used in interfaces to compensate for bus access delays, or within interfaces. Buffers may be dedicated to a particular device or may be issued by a buffer manager component of the operating system on an as-needed basis.

6.2 Cacheing – Its Effect on System Throughput and Hardware Usage

The way in which disk I/O takes place on any system is a critical factor in its performance. Therefore it is of the utmost importance that it be as fast and efficient as possible. A number of ways exist to optimise the transfer of information to and from disk; some of these methods involve faster and more complex hardware, and others utilise larger bodies of software to maintain a cacheing system of disk information most frequently accessed by the system.

In the first case more hardware is bought, usually involving a fast bus-type configuration on the transfer highway between the disk subsystem and the processor's memory, almost always with some memory buffering between the disk transfer highway and the bus on which the processor memory lives.

The second method of speeding throughput is by adding a cacheing system. In cacheing systems frequently accessed material is brought from disk to memory and kept in a reserved area of memory called cache; this may be part of the computer's memory, or some special high speed memory. Thereafter any I/O requests for the cached information are trapped (sometimes by special hardware or else by extra operating system code), and the information supplied from the cache. Types of information held in a cache vary and are often selectable. The types which it is of the greatest advantage to cache are as follows:

1) Directories, especially master or root directories.
2) System overlays – though this implies a badly built system.
3) User data (advantageous in data base system applications).
4) Programs which may be accessed by many users very frequently, as, for example, a menu program might be in a commercial user environment.

Many systems operate a "Residency quantum" cache, which is a complex way of saying that the cached information is overwritten after a fixed period of remaining unaccessed to make way for new information to be cached. The way in which a cache is implemented is obviously highly machine dependent, and its efficiency will vary greatly from machine to machine. In the general case there is always a large benefit to throughput by an effective use of the available cacheing mechanisms.

Now to take the classes of information listed for cacheing in detail.

1. Directories: On any user disk the top of the tree directory is always likely to be a very frequently accessed item of data, containing as it does the links to all lesser order directories, and in many cases the actual disk information (e.g. on RSTS disks the status word and disk ID reside in the master directories).

Given this frequent access factor it is obviously going to make a dent in the system performance if the master directory information has to be fetched for every single file access. Accordingly when a cache is implemented the master (or root) directory is a prime candidate for keeping in it. The way in which the cacheing of this item usually works is that it is loaded into cache at system startup time and is then only written back to disk when the copy of it held in cache is altered. Since most of the accesses are to find the links to user directories, they read only information from the master directory, and no disk update is necessary. The case where a user directory is deleted or added, resulting in the need for a disk update, is comparatively rare. On a system like RSTS, where the master file directory contains some accounting information, updates would be more frequent. In any case the disk I/O is liable to be a great deal less suitable for this purpose.

2) System Overlays: A general requirement of any operating system is that it should provide maximum facilities whilst consuming the minimum of the available resources of the system. A part of this is that it should be as small a body of machine code as possible. Whilst all the operating system's facilities are required by someone somewhere, it is quite probable that a few of them may only be used occasionally. In this case a technique of overlay coding is used. What this means in plain English, is that when a user types in a command which is perhaps not used very frequently, the operating system will claw back some memory from the user area and fetch in from disk the program segment(s) required to implement it. After the command is executed the memory is handed back to the memory manager for users again. In some cases the cache can be used to retain this program code, though to gain any great benefit from cacheing this information, it should be frequently accessed, and this in turn implies that the command involved is often used and should be part of the main body of the operating system anyway.

3) User Data: This kind of information is most eligible for cacheing when a system is in use as a data base, rather than in mainly computational applications. This is because a whole group of users may be accessing different sections of the same large data file all day every day. When this situation occurs, the cache can keep the most recently read sections of the file, obviating many disk accesses.

4) Programs: When a program is run by many users there may be an advantage in keeping a copy of it in cache, if many users are loading and reloading it. This is due to the obvious speed advantage in doing memory-to-memory copies over disk I/O. Where a single copy of a program may be used by many users (pure code or re-entrant code) this will gain no advantage.

6.3 Spool Programs

The name SPOOL is an acronym of the phrase "Simultaneous Peripheral Operation On-Line", and as such is perhaps a misnomer. The kind of peripherals with which SPOOL programs are often concerned are printers, and it is not possible to use a printer for several different users simultaneously, unless they do not mind one another's printout being intermingled , which seems hardly likely. Printer SPOOL programs (SPOOLers) act as managers for the devices which they control. The usual arrangement is to have one SPOOLer per print device. This will receive requests from system users for files to be printed and will keep in a disk file a list of all these requests, printing files required one after another until the list is exhausted. The contents of this file may be one of a number of things:

1) A list of file names and the directories under which they are stored.

2) A list of SPOOL files containing copies of the actual files to be printed: this is a useful feature where the files to be printed are being constantly accessed or updated. Using this arrangement the SPOOL files must be deleted after they are printed, and this can have dangers, as we shall discuss shortly.

3) A list of files to be printed, with details about the kind of stationery they are to be printed upon, and any special parameters to be applied in formatting the output.

Why then are SPOOL programs of such great value? In hardware terms a printer with its various mechanical parts – hammers, print wires, ribbon mechanisms, print band, print drum, carriage, and so on for various types, represents a high fault liability. This applies to all printers, especially large ones, due to their vibrational characteristics, and general mechanical and electronic complexity. Therefore printers are expensive to buy and maintain. Where buyers of minicomputers are concerned, this often means that a single printer is bought for each category of printing to be done. One large printer for volume medium quality output (program listings, stock listings, mailing lists, for example), one small dot matrix printer for small volume medium quality output (internal memos, address labels, account results, for example) and one so called "letter quality" or "typewriter quality" printer for high quality medium volume printing, like word-processed letters or documentation. The most intensively used of these types is almost certain to be the large printer, typically being in use for half of each working day as an average. If users were allowed to simply output to a printer of this type for whatever they wanted, there would be endless conflicts between users, as the operating system would only allow one user at a time to assign the printer for use. Using this first-come-first-served approach, users would have to wait for the printer to be free before they could continue, not a very efficient use of the user's time, and since the printer is only printing in fits and starts, not a very efficient use of the printer. If a SPOOLer is added, the main SPOOL program can be running all the time as a user job, but not attached to any terminal. This program can print all the files in its queue and can receive messages from a "front end" program which users can run. This front end program will prompt the user to enter what he wants printed along with any other information required, and having obtained this it will pass a message, via a system facility or a disk file, to the main SPOOL program. Users now submit their requests, then get on with other things, and the printer now has a continuous stream of files to print.

SPOOLer programs can provide a great many additional facilities. A few examples are listed below:

1) Formatting the output according to parameters contained in parameter files to effect printing in boxes on preprinted stationery, or other strictly positioned items.

2) Timed printing: it may be required to start a print in the middle of the night after some file has been updated. This allows the SPOOL program to take the place of a human operator.

3) Confirmation messages: a message may be sent to the user who requested the print along the lines of: "Message from SPOOLer: your printout of file SALES.DAT is now available".

4) Header prints to assist in segregating different printouts. Most SPOOLer programs print the name of the file in very large letters before the file.

5) Multi copies: most SPOOLers will allow a number of copies to be specified. This is useful where something like the company's accounts or a sales report has to be circulated between many executives or departments.

In the general case, SPOOL programs must be able to be halted and restarted to allow the printer to be freed for uses other than normal printing – like the running of engineers' test print programs. Another vital ability is not losing any output if the printer drops offline, due to running out of paper, etc. If a printer fault goes unnoticed the SPOOLer deletes the copies of the files it has to print, as it prints them; there may be no possibility of reprinting a file which was printed incorrectly. This will certainly be the case where the system application programs generate their output to SPOOL files, a lengthy re-run may be possible, but is not ideal. A far better arrangement is where the SPOOL files are only deleted on the approval of the system manager or operator.

There are several hardware implications to using SPOOLer programs. First is the fact that printer usage is heavy, and more importantly, continuous. Continual usage of any machine can throw up heat problems that might never happen when the same machine was subjected to the same amount of usage spread out into small bursts. This kind of fault is often caused by overheating driver transistors, or power supply components which are strictly speaking faulty, but can function adequately when cool. Secondly, there has been another level added between the user and the printer which is, as far as the operating system is concerned, an additional job. The SPOOL programs can be affected by malfunctions in the system just like any other user program, and can cease to function. If someone now requests – via the front end SPOOL program – that a file be printed, nothing happens. After a time, the inexperienced user may conclude that the printer itself is faulty; thus the existence of the SPOOL program has successfully hoodwinked the user as to the real nature of the fault.

6.4 Setting Up the Job Priorities

In the final analysis a given computer has a finite throughput which cannot be exceeded. The trick of maximum efficiency in computing is in ensuring that all the various components are as efficient as possible. This includes the operating system, the user application programs, the file store (see Chapter Four, Section D), and the hardware. Within the operating system section there are a number of things which can be done to streamline the running of the system. We shall be looking in more detail at some of these in Chapter Seven. In this section we shall examine the more subjective concept of response times. So far as a system user is concerned, a response time is the greatest measure of a computer's speed and efficiency. Response time may be defined as the time it takes the computer to respond to a command typed in at a terminal. Take the following examples: in each case the response time will be considered as being from the moment when the commands typed in are finished by a line terminator, and when the requested information appears on the screen.

EXAMPLES:

1) RSX — type in "PIP/DI" plus a carriage return.
2) VMS — type in "DIR" plus a carriage return.
3) RSTS — type in "CAT" plus a carriage return.

When the user is performing data entry, terminal response times can become critical, as the repetitive nature of such work means that the operator knows the data entry sequence by heart and can anticipate what will be required next. If the response times are slow, the user may type in the data before it is prompted for, and, if the system responses are severely degraded, may get so far ahead that silly mistakes are made. Where possible, it is a better idea to build system application packages so that data entry programs create small files of manageable length to temporarily store data entry in, and then run some merging procedure at a slack time of day such as lunchtime or overnight, which will incorporate the newly entered data into the main data files. This way of performing data input will enable the data entry programs to be run at a higher priority than other jobs on the system, which will probably reduce the user's frustration and also the possibility of mistakes occurring. It is true that doing this will slow down the non-terminal jobs, but since data input programs spend a fair percentage of their time waiting for keyboard input (including the time when characters are being typed in, but a line terminator has not yet been entered) the degradation should not be serious, as when the terminal jobs run they do so in short bursts. A great deal of experimentation would be needed to implement such a scheme as this, because the correct relative priorities would have to be established, so as not to degrade the non-terminal jobs excessively. The error logger should, as previously mentioned, be the highest priority job on the system at all times. The error logger will hopefully spend most of its time inactive in any case, so that giving it this high priority will have little or no effect on the rest of the system.

One other point about prioritising users.... if the scheme outlined above is not applicable or not implementable on a given system a number of other ways can be found within user level programs to make them more efficient which will, if sufficient computing power is available, tackle the problem at source. First avoid any unnecessary program opening or closing of files; this will minimise the directory search overhead. Read any available literature from the software company which supplied your language package on the subject of good programming style and overhead minimisation.

Where all jobs run at the same priority there will not be any difference in the CPU time allotted to each, resulting in poor responses and user annoyance. In a really bad case purely system jobs like SPOOL programs can eat into system performance to an unacceptable degree, thus making the whole system slow even when they are not in use. The details of prioritising depend upon the operating system, the types of job going on the system and the importance attached to each individual job by the system manager.

6.5 Language Support

Whilst an operating system is a very powerful piece of software, it is only a means to an end. The end in this case is the running of programs to process data in some way. The operating system only provides the environment in which these user programs can run. It does not provide a programming language in which to write them. Therefore, grafted on to most operating systems there is at least one programming language system. These systems are usually separate in minicomputers, but in a few cases are amalgamated into one body of software. Even language systems which are considered separate from their host operating systems are highly dependent on them. This dependence mainly takes the form of allowing system information to be used by user programs, and also on I/O from disks, terminals and printers.

We shall look now at the BASIC-PLUS language system used with RSTS. In this case BASIC-PLUS acts as a kind of backstop input interpreter; thus, if RSTS cannot resolve what a user types in as a valid RSTS command, the BASIC-PLUS run time system attempts to recognise it. Of course, if neither recognise the input, then the "? WHAT ?" error message appears on the screen. Many items of system information are available to programs written in BASIC-PLUS. Listed below are a few statements and an explanatory note about what they will do.

"PRINT DATE$(0)"	prints out the date today.
"PRINT TIME$(0)"	prints out the system clock.
"PRINT POS(0)"	prints out the value of the character position at which the next character will appear on the line at the terminal.
"KILL 'TRYST.OCC'"	causes the RSTS file processor to delete the file "TRYST.OCC" – if it exists.

"PRINT TIME(0)" prints out the number of seconds which have elapsed since the system was started up.

When a user uses the "OLD" command to load a BASIC-PLUS source file what happens is that his area of memory contains the code generated by the BASIC-PLUS compiler to implement the statements it sees coming in, line by line, from the source file. A temporary file is created to house a copy of the source file. This sequence of events, when completed, leaves an executable image of the program in the user's area of memory, and the copy of the source file which BASIC-PLUS will edit as statements are added or deleted in the course of program development. The "COMPILE" command can then be used at any time when the user wants to save an executable image to disk; this will write the contents of his memory into a file with a ".BAC" extension. If the source file is altered in any way the new source version can be made to supercede the old version, using the "REPLACE" command.

The drawbacks of the system, and indeed any system like it, are that, first, it relies very heavily on support from the run time system. The compiled version of the program is not a stand-alone program because it needs the library of subroutines and support from RSTS and the BASIC-PLUS run time system. This rather limits anybody who wants to produce a truly stand-alone program for any purpose. Compiled programs do load and run far more quickly than source programs, but if bugs are discovered in the program, errors will be reported in exactly the same way as if the source were being used — for example, "Data format error at line 2100". If the compiled version is being run, however, there will be no way of listing out the program to de-bug it.

For time-sharing systems BASIC-PLUS is a very good system, highly interactive and very easy to use, but if you need to produce stand-alone programs, it is not of any use.

CHAPTER 7
The Mysterious Case of the Slow System

7.1 System Monitoring

A slow system is one which is performing its job at a speed below its capabilities. This may be evident by fixed length tasks taking longer than they should, or by slow responses to terminal input. In this context, the word "system" will be taken to encompass the hardware, the operating system and the application software. Any of these three system components may, singly or interactively, present an obstacle to maximum throughput, or perceived system speed.

System speed slows down gradually in some cases. This may be over a period of months, and be so insidious that a great deal of time may elapse before the speed degradation becomes such that some remedial action is attempted. In other cases, a system may considerably slow down within a very short space of time. This second case is liable to lead to an immediate investigation. Take the case where a system has been bought and installed. The machine is to be used for two major purposes, employee details and their pay calculation, and also for the general company accounting. The employee details and payroll applications package is available off the shelf. The company accounting package is, however, a special case and a bespoke software package has to be developed for the machine. The personnel and payroll department users are on the machine from the installation date. After a few months the accounting package is ready, and over one weekend it is installed. On the following Monday, the personnel and payroll department log on to the system, and realise that the system is noticeably slower. The accounts department users have just started using the system, so they don't know any different, and accept the "new" speed at which the machine appears to run. Thus, we now have the original users, who have been used to one speed, and will now probably remark or complain about the new speed. We also have the newly-added users, who are oblivious to the fact that the system is in fact capable of providing faster processing of their tasks. This "perceived speed" factor in assessing system performance is important. In the example just described the actual throughput of the machine has been increased – it now has more user data to process. The external appearance to one user, however, is that the system is slower. In extreme cases, of course, when adding more users brings "perceived speed" down to unacceptable levels, the options are to streamline the applications software, fine-tune the operating system, or to buy a faster hardware configuration, e.g. upgrade the CPU type. This will hold true only if the existing hardware is found to be fully extended. A more insidious slowdown in system responses and timed task execution can often be found to be due to the file structure fragmentation covered in chapter 4 section D.

When investigating slow systems, it is important to realise the difference between a system which is over-extended, and one which is merely inefficient. In the case of an over-extended system, too little computing and I/O capacity are being shared between too many users to be able to provide either a fast "perceived speed" or actual throughput speed. In the case of an inefficient system some hardware or software factor is wasting the available computing power and I/O capacity.

The greatest aids to making an assessment of any particular system's efficiency are the system monitor utilities provided with almost all operating systems. These user level programs interrogate system performance data and format it into output for use in diagnosing the inefficiencies. In addition, these programs are used to assess the effect of combative measures taken against these same inefficiencies.

7.2 The System Monitor Programs

The system monitor programs for our three example operating systems are listed below. In all three cases they show who is using the system, general system states and resource levels, and a wealth of other system details.

RSX = "RMD". This utility shows the state of the RSX system. The memory usage details and the system partitions and other system details.

VMS = "Monitor". Shows a large selection of system details on nine separately selectable displays. Using "Monitor" a very detailed, very complex picture of the VMS operating system and the system hardware can be built up.

RSTS = "SYSTAT". The Systat utility shows the users, resources, general state and file access information for a RSTS system. The major difference between Systat and the other two monitoring utilities mentioned above is that it is not a single screen full of information, updated for dynamic monitoring of the system. (Other RSTS utilities like "STATUS" are used for this type of monitoring.)

All these three programs are specifically provided for the purpose of monitoring the current system status and its overall efficiency. "SYSTAT" is less geared toward system tuning than the other two, but as we shall be concentrating on other programs to do with RSTS tuning in section B of this chapter, this is of no consequence.

The System Monitor Programs: RSX – "RMD" and ATL command.

The RSX "RMD" utility is designed to give a dynamic display of certain items of information on a suitable DEC or DEC-compatible VDU terminal. The method of invoking it varies, but once it is running, the following major items of interest are:

    The amount of free space on the disks in use.
    The size of the system buffer pool.
    The names of the system partitions.
    The overall memory size.
    The number of error sequences which have occurred.
    A map of the memory, showing the usage of it.

```
RSX-11M V4.0 BL32      (VISTA )  512K              10-NOV-83 16:40:58
TASK=  *IDLE*              FREE=   SYO:35105.
                                   DP1:27627.                   PARS
POOL=8962.:9108.:15.
     8962.:9108.:15.                                         EXCOM1:C
                                                             EXCOM2:C
IN:   EET MFF    R    PR    QLL                              LDRPAR:T
9     XXT CC1    E    MM    MPP                              TTPAR :T
33K   CC: RS1    S    TD    G01                              DRVPAR:D
OUT:  OO  .RA    R    .T    .                                SYSPAR:T
0     MM  .EC    M    .1    .                                FCSRES:C
OK    12  .SP    S    .4    .                                FCPPAR:D
      !!-)>!->------!>-> <>>>                                RESRMS:C
0*******32******64******96******128*****160*****192*****224*****   GEN   :D
EP---CT-TCD-C------D----------------------------------------
------------------------------------------------------------
256*****288*****320*****352*****384*****416*****448*****480*****

                                                             ERRSEQ
                                                             0.
```

Figure 7.1

114

```
ATL
LDR... 117510  LDRPAR 117624 00142400-00145200  Pri - 248.  Dpri - 248.
    Status:  -CHK FXD STP -PMD PRV NSD
    TI - COO:  IOC - O.  BIO - O.  Eflg - 000001 000000  PS - 170000
    PC - 120354 Regs 0-6 120212 007527 177777 062326 060014 062274 120166
MCR... 113004  SYSPAR 116434 00213400-00223500  Pri - 160.  Dpri - 160.
    Status:  STP -PMD PRV CLI NSD CAL
    TI - TTO:  IOC - O.  BIO - O.  Eflg - 000001 040000  PS - 170000
    PC - 122462 Regs 0-6 000000 120476 122056 120432 010354 032740 120366
MCRTO 062274  GEN    060014 00553700-00573700  Pri - 160.  Dpri - 160.
    Status:  -CHK CKD -PMD REM PRV MCR
    TI - TTO:  IOC - O.  BIO - O.  Eflg - 000001 040000  PS - 170000
    PC - 121502 Regs 0-6 120424 121324 121734 000000 121330 000000 000762
REGLOA 040454  GEN    035744 00500700-00516300  Pri - 150.  Dpri - 150.
    Status:  STP -PMD
    TI - COO:  IOC - O.  BIO - O.  Eflg - 000001 000000  PS - 170000
    PC - 013550 Regs 0-6 000512 067000 001014 001034 000061 000670 000266
F11ACP 116100  FCPPAR 036340 00255400-00301400  Pri - 149.  Dpri - 149.
    Status:  STP ACP -PMD PRV NSD CAL
    TI - COO:  IOC - O.  BIO - O.  Eflg - 000002 040002  PS - 170000
    PC - 121156 Regs 0-6 000000 047410 000000 117174 037034 047410 120314
PMT... 113350  GEN    035500 00472400-00500700  Pri - 148.  Dpri - 148.
    Status:  STP -PMD PRV CAL
    TI - COO:  IOC - O.  BIO - O.  Eflg - 000100 000000  PS - 170000
    PC - 121736 Regs 0-6 000074 000102 000000 140164 157700 000000 120212
QMG... 115650  GEN    035434 00601500-00633700  Pri - 75.  Dpri - 75.
    Status:  STP -PMD PRV
    TI - COO:  IOC - O.  BIO - O.  Eflg - 000000 000000  PS - 170000
    PC - 120644 Regs 0-6 126310 123356 122376 000456 000000 000001 120406
LP0   115170  GEN    037560 00633700-00647700  Pri - 70.  Dpri - 70.
    Status:  STP -PMD PRV SLV
    TI - COO:  IOC - O.  BIO - O.  Eflg - 000600 140000  PS - 170000
    PC - 121022 Regs 0-6 121702 122014 000052 127250 130621 000001 120416
LP1   043274  GEN    036010 00647700-00663700  Pri - 70.  Dpri - 70.
    Status:  WFR -PMD PRV SLV
    TI - COO:  IOC - 1.  BIO - O.  Eflg - 000201 140000  PS - 170010
    PC - 132010 Regs 0-6 000011 131441 000002 131452 126500 000002 120352
TT3   043410  GEN    044360 00663700-00677700  Pri - 70.  Dpri - 70.
    Status:  STP WFR -PMD PRV SLV
    TI - COO:  IOC - O.  BIO - 1.  Eflg - 000407 140000  PS - 170010
    PC - 130422 Regs 0-6 121702 130535 000010 127256 130545 000015 120412
VIST7 046034  GEN    070350 01731000-02010000  Pri - 50.  Dpri - 50.
    Status:  WFR -PMD REM
    TI - TT7:  IOC - O.  BIO - O.  Eflg - 000004 100000  PS - 170000
    PC - 117206 Regs 0-6 000004 000013 004400 002376 000001 000000 000502
VIST11 045644  GEN    063040 00677700-00737000  Pri - 50.  Dpri - 50.
    Status:  STP WFR -PMD REM
    TI - TT11:  IOC - O.  BIO - 1.  Eflg - 000004 100000  PS - 170000
    PC - 117206 Regs 0-6 000024 000025 004400 002376 177705 000000 000502
VIST2 053724  GEN    063334 01054400-01113500  Pri - 50.  Dpri - 50.
    Status:  STP WFR -PMD REM
    TI - TT2:  IOC - O.  BIO - 1.  Eflg - 000004 100000  PS - 170000
    PC - 117206 Regs 0-6 000024 000025 004400 002376 177705 000000 000502
VIST5 052734  GEN    047654 01434700-01452400  Pri - 50.  Dpri - 50.
    Status:  STP WFR -PMD REM
    TI - TT5:  IOC - O.  BIO - O.  Eflg - 000004 100000  PS - 170000
    PC - 117206 Regs 0-6 000003 000004 004400 002376 177734 000000 000502
VIST1 063150  GEN    050764 01221100-01260200  Pri - 50.  Dpri - 50.
    Status:  STP WFR -PMD REM MCR
    TI - TT1:  IOC - O.  BIO - O.  Eflg - 000004 100000  PS - 170000
    PC - 117206 Regs 0-6 000004 000005 004400 002376 177665 000000 000502
VIST4 065174  GEN    060060 01271500-01350600  Pri - 50.  Dpri - 50.
    Status:  STP WFR -PMD REM
    TI - TT4:  IOC - O.  BIO - 1.  Eflg - 000004 100000  PS - 170000
    PC - 117206 Regs 0-6 000024 000025 004400 002376 177711 000000 000502
VIST13 061750  GEN    065654 00516300-00534000  Pri - 50.  Dpri - 50.
    Status:  STP WFR -PMD REM MCR
    TI - TT13:  IOC - O.  BIO - 1.  Eflg - 000004 100000  PS - 170000
    PC - 117206 Regs 0-6 000120 000120 004400 002376 000001 000000 000502
VIST14 055220  GEN    056474 00534000-00553700  Pri - 50.  Dpri - 50.
    Status:  STP WFR -PMD REM MCR
    TI - TT14:  IOC - O.  BIO - 1.  Eflg - 000004 100000  PS - 170000
    PC - 117206 Regs 0-6 000003 000004 004400 002376 177676 000000 000502
VIST15 061464  GEN    062654 00737000-01007300  Pri - 50.  Dpri - 50.
    Status:  -PMD REM MCR
    TI - TT15:  IOC - O.  BIO - O.  Eflg - 000005 100000  PS - 170004
    PC - 121022 Regs 0-6 037251 000022 000034 000000 003000 063264 000504
```

Figure 7.1a

The printout shown in Figure 7.1 is from a PDP-11/34 system, which has had extra hardware added to it, to allow usage of 512kw of memory. There are two disks in use on the system. First, the system disk – SYO:, and DPl:. There have been no errors detected on the system. The various system components are shown. These include RMD itself, the MCR console monitor, RMS,LP0 and LP1 (this system has two line printers). At the time this printout was taken the system was very lightly loaded, but by watching this display update when the system is heavily loaded, a great deal of information may be gleaned about what the RSX 11M operating system is doing. The current task is also shown, and we can see that at the time this printout was taken, the system was idle.

For obtaining more details on RSX systems, the Active Task List is very useful. This is invoked by typing "ATL", and shows the following information about each active task:

The task name.
The CPU register – including the program counter – values which will be used during the next runburst of the task.
The current, and default, priority level of the task.
The terminal with which the task is associated (RSX terminals are numbered in octal; e.g. TT10 is the eighth terminal).
The status of the task (e.g. if it is checkpointed or not)

Figure 7.1a is a printout resulting from an "ATL" command. By taking these two sources of information, along with program statistics, the RSX system performance and status may be monitored.

The VMS "Monitor" Program

The VMS MONITOR program is invoked by typing in "MON XXX" at a logged-in terminal. The XXX part of the command will contain one of the following classnames:

1) DECNET
2) FCP
3) IO
4) LOCK
5) MODES
6) PAGE
7) POOL
8) PROCESSES
9) STATES

The selected classname will be displayed. If you run "MONITOR" on a VDU, rather than a hard copy terminal, the data will overwrite itself at each successive update, giving a dynamic status display for the selected class of information. If, for example, you need to see the system users and follow their progress, type "MON PROCESS/INT=10" at a logged-in terminal. This will result in a display of the currently active processes on the system and the details about each. The display will be updated at intervals of ten seconds. Of the available nine classes, we shall examine four in more detail. (Incidentally, to exit from MONITOR type CTRL/Y – CTRL and Y keys simultaneously.)

"MON PAGE/INT=10" will invoke the PAGE display. VAX memory under the VAX memory management hardware is partitioned into ½K pages. Any time a page must be swapped in or out to disk or cache, a page fault is said to occur. This page faulting mechanism is a very powerful feature of the VAX, but needs careful control by VMS. If too great an amount of page-swapping is going on, then the overall system will suffer. Thus it is of great importance to ensure that the incidence of page faults be as low as possible. The PAGE display shows the various statistics associated with the paging function. Information displayed includes things like the overall rate of page faults, the amount of pages read and written to disk and the incidence of pages which were faulted at the same time they were being swapped. Figure 7.2 shows the PAGE display.

```
                    VAX/VMS MONITOR UTILITY
                  PAGE MANAGEMENT STATISTICS
                       19-OCT-1983
                        10:03:12

                              CUR       AVE       MIN       MAX

PAGE FAULT RATE              25.79     10.68      0.00     35.79
PAGE READ RATE                0.00      0.00      0.00      0.40
PAGE READ I/O RATE            0.00      0.00      0.00      0.20
PAGE WRITE RATE               0.00      1.81      0.00     95.23

PAGE WRITE I/O RATE           0.00      0.01      0.00      0.99
FREE LIST FAULT RATE          7.80      3.30      0.00     12.60
MODIFIED LIST FAULT RATE     18.00      7.29      0.00     25.00
DEMAND ZERO FAULT RATE        0.00      0.07      0.00      0.60
GLOBAL VALID FAULT RATE       0.00      0.00      0.00      0.00

WRT IN PROGRESS FAULT RATE    0.00      0.00      0.00      0.00
SYSTEM FAULT RATE             0.00      0.02      0.00      1.00
FREE LIST SIZE             5974.00   5861.43   5654.00   6146.00
MODIFIED LIST SIZE          147.00    231.75      1.00    426.00
```

Figure 7.2

117

"MON MODES/INT=10" is the command to invoke the modes display. This displays in a bar graph format, the number of clock ticks which the processor has spent in each of its possible seven modes. (In this context one clock tick represents 1/10th of one second.) The seven modes are:

1) Interrupt stack — indicates how much time has been spent processing interrupts since the last sample began.

2) Kernel mode — shows the amount of time spent executing VMS kernel code in the current sample period (i.e. since the last screen update).

3) EXECUTIVE mode — this value indicates the amount of time spent in executive mode (e.g. executing RMS code).

4) SUPERVISOR mode — this indicates the supervisory time spent executing things like DCL code (for input parsing, etc.).

5) USER mode — time spent executing VAX instructions for user programs.

6) COMPATIBILITY mode — as the PDP-11 instruction set is a subset of the standard VAX instruction set, it is compatible with PDP-11 when the VAX is placed in Compatibility mode. This value indicates how much time has been expended executing such instructions.

7) IDLE time — shows how much of the current sample period was spent with the processor idle. Defined as the amount of time spent executing the NULL process because there was nothing useful to be done.

The MODES display is as shown in Figure 7.3

"MON IO/INT=10" initiates a display of the system I/O statistics, resampled every ten seconds. This will display fourteen items of information. In common with other classes, the current, maximum, minimum and average figures for the sampled values are displayed. The fourteen displayed are:

1) The direct IO rate, which shows the amount of disk and tape IO activity.
2) The buffered IO rate — terminal and printer rates.
3) Mailbox write rate — the amount of message passing between processes.

```
                                 VAX/VMS MONITOR UTILITY
            +-----+              TIME IN PROCESSOR MODES
            \ CUR \                  19-OCT-1983
            +-----+                    09:58:29

                                  0         25        50        75       100
                                  + - - - + - - - + - - - + - - - + - - - +
INTERRUPT STACK               5 \**         \         \         \         \
                                  \          \         \         \         \
KERNEL MODE                  51 \********************         \         \
                                  \          \         \         \         \
EXECUTIVE MODE               36 \***************         \         \
                                  \          \         \         \         \
SUPERVISOR MODE                   \          \         \         \         \
                                  \          \         \         \         \
USER MODE                     6 \**         \         \         \         \
                                  \          \         \         \         \
COMPATIBILITY MODE                \          \         \         \         \
                                  \          \         \         \         \
IDLE TIME                         \          \         \         \         \
                                  \          \         \         \         \
                                  + - - - + - - - + - - - + - - - + - - - +
```

Figure 7.3

```
PROCESS COUNT: 10           VAX/VMS MONITOR UTILITY        UPTIME:   0 18:46:54
                                    PROCESSES
                                   21-OCT-1983
                                    09:04:29

   PID       UIC      STATE PRI   NAME        SIZE      DIOCNT  FAULTS  CPU TIME

00010000 [000,000] COM    0 NULL          0/0          0        0 18:00:25.0
00010001 [000,000] HIB   16 SWAPPER       0/0          0        0 00:00:04.9
001B0016 [106,005] LEF    9 POLICY        0/175       16      202 00:00:01.8
000C0017 [001,004] CUR    6 SYSTEM       28/180     5284     8020 00:03:05.8
00010018 [001,004] HIB    6 HALOS        12/155   505361     3962 00:21:31.0
00010019 [001,004] LEF    8 OPCOM         0/76         2       45 00:00:00.1
0001001A [001,004] HIB   10 JOB_CONTROL  43/114      142       80 00:00:02.4
000A001B [001,004] HIB    8 PRTSYMB1      0/15        17      220 00:00:09.0
0001001C [001,003] HIB   10 DMAOBACP     52/117     5567     1601 00:01:33.1
0002001D [001,006] HIB    7 ERRFMT        0/45       238       60 00:00:03.5
```

Figure 7.4

```
                            VAX/VMS MONITOR UTILITY
                             I/O SYSTEM STATISTICS
                                  19-OCT-1983
                                   10:06:23
```

	CUR	AVE	MIN	MAX
DIRECT I/O RATE	219.70	260.30	219.70	277.79
BUFFERED I/O RATE	0.00	0.02	0.00	0.20
MAILBOX WRITE RATE	0.00	0.00	0.00	0.00
WINDOW TURN RATE	0.00	0.00	0.00	0.00
LOG NAME TRANSLATION RATE	9.02	2.56	0.00	9.02
FILE OPEN RATE	0.00	0.00	0.00	0.00
PAGE FAULT RATE	3.94	3.57	2.79	4.59
PAGE READ RATE	0.00	0.08	0.00	0.60
PAGE READ I/O RATE	0.00	0.02	0.00	0.20
PAGE WRITE RATE	0.00	0.00	0.00	0.00
PAGE WRITE I/O RATE	0.00	0.00	0.00	0.00
INSWAP RATE	0.00	0.00	0.00	0.00
FREE LIST SIZE	5633.00	5593.50	5581.00	5633.00
MODIFIED LIST SIZE	392.00	380.00	362.00	393.00

Figure 7.5

4) Window turns – this is a measure of the directory efficiency of the disks.
5) Logical name translation – indicates references to logical names for files or devices.
6) File open rate – the rate at which files are being opened.
7) Page fault rate – as for the PAGE display definition.
8) Page read rate – the number of pages read into memory from disk.
9) Page read I/O rate – the amount of disk reading for page faults.
10) Page write rate – amount of disk writes for page swapouts.
11) Page write I/O rate – the amount of disk I/Os to write pages to disk.
12) Inswap rate – the rate at which working sets of page lists are being read in from disk from the swapping file.
13) Free list size – number of free pages held in the Free Page List.
14) Modified list size – number of pages contained in the modified page list.

Figure 7.4 is an example of the IO display. In systems which are I/O bound, this display will greatly assist in any attempts at improvement. We shall look at how this may be done in the next section of this chapter.

"MON PROCESS/INT=10" is the command to see a display of the current processes on the system. Especially useful to the system manager, this display shows not only the user processes, but also the state of system processes like the "NULL" process, which is executed when the scheduler cannot find anything else ready to run, and the "SWAPPER" process. Most importantly, the general details of each process are shown. These include the name, priority, size and the process identification number (PID) of each process. All of these items are useful for various kinds of system tuning and its day-to-day monitoring. Figure 7.5 is an example run from the command given above.

RSTS: SYSTAT.

The RSTS system status monitor program interrogates the RSTS monitor tables to extract various types of information. By logging into the 1,2 system library account and typing, "RUN SYSTAT", you get the "OUTPUT STATUS TO?" question. If you want the status report at your own terminal, type carriage return; otherwise type the name of the device (e.g. "LP:" is the system line printer), or the file to which you want to output the report. Also available at this point is the option of seeing only portions of the report. For example, if you only want to see the disk structure section of the report, type "/D", then return, or "/S" for just the jobs. "/B" will show the busy devices, and "/C" will, on version 7.0 or later, show the memory usage map. The jobs report shows the user's account, the terminal he is using, the program that the user is running and the state of the job. Additionally, the amount of CPU time is shown, and the priority and runburst setting for each user are shown. The disk structure shows the disk size, the number of free blocks left on it, the number of files currently open on it and the number of errors which have been detected in its usage since the system was last started. Additionally, the percentage of the disk space which is free is also shown, along with the volume name for the particular pack currently on the drive. This information is shown for each disk mounted (i.e. recognised) by the system. Figure 7.6 shows the output from "SYSTAT" obtained by typing "/SBDF" in response to the "OUTPUT STATUS TO?" question. (For those readers familiar with RSTS, typing "SYS /SBDF" from the "Ready" prompt will have the same effect where there is a CCL defined for SYSTAT.)

```
RSTS V7.2-04 RSTS SYSTEM  STATUS AT 03-NOV-83, 14:10    UP: 34:19:49

JOB   WHO      WHERE   WHAT     SIZE    STATE      RUN-TIME  PRI/RB   RTS
 1   [SELF]    DET     ERRCPY   5/31K   SR D16       12.6     0/6    BASIC
 2   [SELF]    DET     OPSRUN   16/31K  SL          5:20.9   -8/6    BASIC
 3   [SELF]    DET     QUMRUN   16/31K  SL          7:26.9    0/6    BASIC
 4   [SELF]    DET     SPLIDL   16/31K  SL D19        1.2    -8/6    BASIC
 5   [SELF]    DET     BATIDL   13/31K  SL D18        0.2    -8/6    BASIC
 7   50,175    KB4     DMRAO2   30/31K  KB          2:22.2   -8/6    ...RSX
 8   50,150    KB6     FDAMO2   31/31K  KB           21.2    -8/6    ...RSX
10   [SELF]    KB0     SYSTAT   13/31K  RN LCK       50.6    -8/6    BASIC
11   50,99     KB2     NONAME   2/31K   ^C           27.9    -8/6    BASIC

BUSY DEVICES: NONE

DISK STRUCTURE:
DSK OPEN      SIZE       FREE    CLU  ERR   NAME    COMMENTS
DP0   26   128000   44924  35%    4    0   SYS000  PUB, DLW
DP1   11   128000   25488  19%    4    0   FINT01  PRI, DLW

GENERAL    FIP                   HUNG
BUFFERS    BUFFERS   JOBS/JOBMAX TTY'S   ERRORS
  450        43        9/20        0        0
```

Figure 7.6

Having looked at the information obtainable from our three sample programs, we will now proceed to look at the interpretation of their outputs, and in the next section we will examine a case study of a RSTS system, using the RSTS system statistical program yet to be introduced.

7.3 Using the system monitor and statistical programs to tune systems.

The whole subject of system tuning is incredibly complex. The amount of effort applied may very often be enormously disproportionate to the improvement obtained. It is always worth trying to assess how far below its capability a system is running, as if the conclusion is "not much", other means of improvement may be explored. The basic premise of tuning an operating system is that all the things it does should be made as streamlined as possible. This may seem an impossible aim when the operating system was written by somebody else, as is the case with almost all systems – very few machine users write their own. Nevertheless, the people who write operating systems have to work on the buckshot principle if they are aiming to sell many licenses to use their products. As mentioned in an earlier context, general purpose operating systems have to be adaptable to many application environments. This implies that many changeable system parameters must be built in, to aid in this tailoring process. This applies not only at the hardware interface level, but also at the user environment level. Comparing a data base with a software development application, it should be evident that the same operating system applied to identical hardware configurations will have to shine at different things in each case. The data base application will require that the disk I/O be performed as efficiently as possible, to facilitate large file searching in reasonable times. The software development machine will need good disk I/O as well, but more importantly it will need fast CPU throughput, as a great deal of compilation will probably be done. Also, in both cases, there will need to be efficient printer handlers. In the first case the printer will probably have to handle large printouts of things like mailing lists, or client details. The hardcopy output in the second case will be used for the various programmers working on the system to print out the intermediate and final versions of their programs under development. This will entail a great deal of short bursts of printing, and as many users will be competing for the use of the printer(s), a SPOOL program will probably be used to handle all print requests. When tuning an operating system, what is the goal at which to aim? The resources of hardware, operating system modules, the CPU and system memory should all be fully, but not over-, used. A point should be sought at which the applications of the system are utilising the hardware (I/O) capability, the CPU time and the memory equally. If any spare capacity exists in any of the three sections, then a way should be sought to use it to relieve another section which is overloaded, e.g. allocating more memory for cache to relieve disk I/O. In practise this delicate balance will be almost impossible to achieve perfectly, and even if reached, may not be stable, since the system and the system storage are dynamic, and changes in some part of a computer system almost always affect some other part.

So now we shall get down to cases, and examine the "SYSTAT" and

"Monitor" programs outlined in the previous section, and look at some ways in which they might aid system tuning.

VMS Monitor

A major part of fine tuning a VMS system is getting the users' working set sizes right. For the uninitiated, each VMS user has what is called a working set of memory pages. Each memory page is 1/2K of memory. The system manager sets the limit of the number of pages which any particular user may occupy, before page swapping must occur. This ensures that the memory is not monopolised by large user processes, and additionally, because user process programs or images are not necessarily all in memory at one time, can prevent wholesale user swapping of the kind which can cripple performance. By observing the running system via a page display of "MONITOR" the size of each user's working set can be slightly adjusted to ascertain what improvement, if any, the change has brought. The overall aim of working set size adjustment is to optimise memory usage. After all, why allow page swapping to occur on a machine with spare memory just because one of two users has reached the limit of his working set? Referring back to Figure 7.2, the seperate headings for page fault rates and page read/write I/O rates show how much of the page fault request total is being satisfied from memory outside the process's working set. Users may examine their working set size by use of the "SHOW WORKING_SET /QUOTA=n" command. The new quota may not exceed the limit authorised by the system manager. Incidentally, the underscore character " " between the words "working" and "set" is set there so that the parser can see the two words as one — which simplifies keyword recognition. In Figure 7.2 the free page pool is shown. As you can see, the number of free pages is high, and during this sample period was slightly higher than average. This sample was taken at a relatively slack time, and the amount of free pages could be expected to drop below this value when system usage is more intense. Also the machine from which this sample was taken had 4m of memory installed.

Progressing now to the processor modes display of Figure 7.3, the amount of spare CPU time shown in this sample is nil. However, this is not always the case, even on a busy system. There will come a time when all processes are awaiting completion of disk I/O or keyboard input, or some other external event. Taken as an average the CPU Idle time will show how much time the processor has spare. If there is hardly any when the system has a full compliment of users logged in, then adding any more users would be futile, since they will only slow down the system. If there is a fair amount of Idle time more users can be allowed on to the computer, so long as the memory and I/O sections of the machine are not running at full capacity already. Adding timed usage is one possibility, with, for example, some users allowed afternoons only. Another useful aid to the system fixer or tuner is the interrupt mode display. If possible, get the system to yourself, then run the monitor modes display as previously described. If there has been a slow system problem, and a noisy terminal is suspected, with no users on the system and only the monitor program running, the interrupt activity should be low. If the interrupt activity is not low, identfication of the errant terminal or terminal line can be easily achieved by briefly disconnecting each terminal line at the CPU back panel in turn until the interrupt mode activity dies down. This will not, of course, isolate any terminal interface faults which are generating spurious interrupts.

The "MONITOR" program IO display can be used for hardware performance tuning, and to find out what sort of ratio of terminal and printer output to disk and magnetic tape I/O is occurring on the system. Why would you need to know this? If it were not possible to differentiate between the terminals and printers and all other kinds of I/O, the job of disk subsystem assessment would be difficult. If the sample period can be guaranteed to be free of magnetic tape usage (which it usually can), a very precise idea of exactly how much disk I/O is being performed can be gained. The knowledge can then be used to assess the efficiency of things like directory cacheing, programs which manipulate large data files can be altered to obtain better figures, an accurate picture can be obtained of which system users are hogging the I/O facilities and, when the information is used properly, it is a very great aid. The amount of files being opened and closed is also shown. This is useful where the repeated opening and closing of files might be a problem. Ways to reduce the open file average can be found, since opening a file also implies a directory search and modification of the file status on the disk. The mailbox rate is a measure of the amount of messages being sent via the RMS (Record Management Services) routines which handle the processing of records within files. The Processes display of monitor will show the relative priorities assigned to each of the active processes on the VMS system. From this display the progress of each process can be monitored. After modifying a program, for example, a programmer may wish to look at the CPU time (see Figure 7.5 for the Processes display). This will aid in making a given program more efficient, and if a program appears to run slowly, by the use of break points the CPU time consumed for each segment of the program can be noted. This will give an accurate idea of which section is most CPU intensive. Taken together with the DIO (Direct I/O) statistics for each process, the efficiency of a program can be observed and, if possble, improved, either by altering the program or the operating system's support of it. The processes display also shows the state of each process, and by keeping a dynamic display active on a VDU the amount of time which each process spends in any particular state can be observed. This will help identify bottlenecks in the system as a whole.

RSTS SYSTAT

SYSTAT is not really designed to be more than a way for a system manager to see who is doing what to the system, and the general state of its resources, but there are a couple of points which can be of use for system speeding. As with the VMS MONITOR utility, there is included in the SYSTAT report the CPU time consumed by each job (see Figure 7.6). Observing this for a particular job will show how fast the job is moving. The second feature is the STATE column. This, like the previous example, will show when the job is waiting for something, and it is possible to diagnose a system as "Disk bound" (see glossary) or "CPU bound" by the regular observation of these states. The actual performance monitoring of RSTS is better performed with a program like "STATUS" which gives a few more facts and figures about the RSTS system, but no details about the current users. "STATUS" is particularly useful because it shows the number of characters output to, or received from, the system's terminals, and the disk read/write statistics.

7.4 Case Study: RSTS QSTATS

The RSTS "QSTATS" program is used to take sample statistics over a long period and format them into a very comprehensive output report. This will break down disk activity into separate types: disk I/O for directory, disk I/O for user data, and so on. Also the efficiency of the cacheing implementation can be ascertained, as well as the general resource levels throughout the sample period. A set of printouts for a QSTATS report are shown as Figures 7.7a through to 7.7f. We shall now examine these statistics and perform interpretation of some of them.

In some values shown the value TIC is used. This is the clock ticks on the machine, derived from the mains frequency. In the United Kingdom this will be 50 ticks per second, and in the USA and elsewhere this will be 60 ticks per second. In the PDP-11 the clock ticks are used to cause clock interrupts (TICS), signalling time to change from the monitor to the user jobs, or vice versa. This gives processor time which can be allocated in known lengths.

	KB.CHAR.IN	KB.CHAR.OUT	DPO:SWAP.R.PHY.CNT	DPO:SWAP.R.PHY.BLK	DPO:SWAP.WRT.CNT
2	14	156	13	768	13
3	18	506	8	396	9
4	9	65	9	496	9
5	11	243	11	592	11
6	11	148	11	592	11
7	11	159	11	576	10
8	12	63	15	792	15
9	63	3830	6	352	6
10	168	2578	8	448	8
11	56	4032	11	640	11
12	65	1688	5	288	5
13	28	2186	12	648	11
14	9	456	12	460	10
15	8	58	11	584	11
16	34	28	13	712	12
17	3	6	10	440	10
18	8	11	9	388	9
19	6	6	6	256	8
20	2	37	5	152	4
MEAN	28.2105	855.579	9.78947	504.211	9.63158
SDEV	9.25282	313.779	.673937	41.2657	.629572

Figure 7.7a

	%SYS.UNCH.TICS	%NULL.TICS	%USER.TICS	%CHARGED.TICS	%UNCHARGED.TICS
2	1.08108	0	16.2162	24.3243	74.3243
3	1.33333	0	29.7778	43.1111	57.7778
4	.465116	0	23.2558	28.3721	72.093
5	1.25	0	33.4375	45.625	54.6875
6	1.69492	0	30.1695	43.3896	55.9322
7	1.17647	0	25.8824	34.902	64.7059
8	2.25806	0	33.2258	41.2903	59.6774
9	.4	0	17.2	34.8	64
10	1.85185	0	26.2963	61.8519	38.8889
11	.615385	0	14.1538	28.9231	70.7692
12	.851064	0	24.2553	51.0638	48.9362
13	3.05085	0	46.1017	67.4576	32.2034
14	3.01867	0	46.0377	56.6038	43.3962
15	1.6	0	54.8	64.4	36
16	1.03448	0	19.6552	28.9655	72.4138
17	2.57143	0	54	64	34.2857
18	2.76923	0	65.7692	72.6154	29.2308
19	1.42857	0	66.4286	73.9286	25
20	34.6341	0	46.3415	45.7805	51.2195
MEAN	3.32026	0	35.4739	46.1266	51.6706
SDEV	1.79781	0	3.69965	3.75507	3.75002

Figure 7.7b

	%FIP.NEEDED	%FIP.IDLE	%FIP.WAITING	%FIP.CODE.WAIT	%FIP.DISK.WAIT
2	49.4595	89.1892	38.1081	0	37.2973
3	54.2222	86.6667	42.6667	1.33333	41.3333
4	58.1395	88.3721	45.5814	0	45.5814
5	45.9375	85.9375	31.25	5	26.25
6	40.339	86.4407	27.4576	0	26.7797
7	40.3922	86.2745	27.8431	0	27.8431
8	23.871	93.5484	16.4516	0	16.4516
9	50.4	82	29.6	0	29.6
10	35.5556	81.4815	18.1481	0	17.037
11	48.9231	81.5385	31.6923	0	31.6923
12	47.234	80.8511	28.9362	1.2766	27.6596
13	27.1186	93.2203	19.322	.338983	18.9831
14	39.2453	84.9057	25.6604	0	24.9057
15	32.4	92	23.2	0	23.2
16	61.0345	84.4828	46.2069	0	46.2069
17	34.8571	92.8571	28	0	26.8571
18	25.2308	95.9231	21.5385	0	19.0769
19	29.6429	92.8571	21.7857	.357143	20.7143
20	51.7073	63.4146	15.6098	0	11.7073
MEAN	41.8795	86.4716	28.3715	.437161	27.3251
SDEV	2.6439	1.72776	2.18817	.277882	2.27979

Figure 7.7c

126

	%FIP.SAT.WAIT	%FIP.OTHER.WAIT	%FIP.CPU	%IO.TIME	%CACHE.TIME
2	.810811	0	11.3514	4.32432	3.51351
3	0	0	11.5556	9.33333	3.11111
4	0	0	12.5581	4.65116	4.18605
5	0	0	14.6875	4.6875	4.6875
6	.677966	0	12.8814	3.05085	2.71186
7	0	0	12.549	2.7451	2.7451
8	0	0	7.41935	3.22581	1.93548
9	0	0	20.8	35.6	3.6
10	1.11111	0	17.4074	40.3704	7.03704
11	0	0	17.2308	28.6154	4.92308
12	0	0	18.2979	26.5106	4.68085
13	0	0	7.79661	24.0678	.677966
14	.754717	0	13.5849	6.41509	6.03774
15	0	0	9.2	4	2.4
16	0	0	14.8276	4.48276	4.48276
17	1.14286	0	6.85714	3.71429	2.57143
18	2.46154	0	3.69231	1.84615	1.53846
19	.714286	0	7.85714	2.14286	2.5
20	3.90244	0	36.0976	.487805	.97561
MEAN	.609249	0	13.508	11.1722	3.38503
SDEV	.241991	0	1.65743	3.04924	.392924

Figure 7.7d

	DPO:OVER.R.CHE.BLK	DPO:DIR.R.PHY.CNT	DPO:DIR.R.PHY.BLK	DPO:DIR.WRT.CNT	D+
2	41	0	0	16	16
3	20	9	9	6	6
4	28	0	0	10	10
5	48	0	0	18	18
6	33	0	0	14	14
7	31	2	2	11	11
8	23	0	0	10	10
9	16	0	0	8	8
10	28	0	0	16	16
11	24	0	0	9	9
12	26	0	0	10	10
13	17	0	0	5	5
14	23	2	2	8	8
15	16	1	1	6	6
16	44	2	2	16	16
17	13	0	0	10	10
18	8	0	0	4	4
19	22	0	0	10	10
20	5	0	0	2	2
MEAN	24.5263	.842105	.842105	9.94737	9.94737
SDEV	2.70044	.498536	.498536	1.04667	1.04667

Figure 7.7e

	DPO:DIR.R.CHE.CNT	DPO:DIR.R.CHE.BLK
2	103	103
3	65	65
4	76	76
5	163	163
6	96	96
7	93	93
8	89	89
9	55	55
10	103	103
11	86	86
12	68	68
13	58	58
14	123	123
15	60	60
16	135	135
17	55	55
18	24	24
19	63	63
20	15	15
MEAN	80.5263	80.5263
SDEV	8.52135	8.52135

Figure 7.7f

Referring first to Figure 7.7a, the rates are shown for the amount of characters input from, and output to, the terminals attached to the system. This shows the amount of I/O for terminals. Figures down the column indicate the number of characters in either direction for each sample period (which in this case was 10 seconds between samples). Nineteen samples were taken, and we can see that the mean average for characters input to the system – shown at the foot of the "KB.CHAR.IN" column – is only 28 characters. On the other hand, the number of characters output peaks at 4032, and at the foot of the "KB.CHAR.IN" column the mean average is shown as 856. From this we can safely conclude that, if this is a typical volume of output, this system would benefit considerably from the replacement of its current terminal interfaces with the less CPU intensive types mentioned later in this chapter. The figures for terminal I/O would tie up with the usage to which this particular system is put, namely word processing, program development and a software library.

And now we move to the swapping statistics section. RSTS swaps whole user areas to memory, but where possible avoids so doing. Any improvements to applications software or system performance parameters to reduce swapping will affect these figures, enabling monitoring of their effectiveness. The "DPO:SWAP.R.PHY.CNT" figures indicate the number of requests received for reads connected with swaps, or loading run time systems, on the disk drive DPO:. The figures in the "DPO:SWAP.R.PHY.BLK" column indicate for the DPO: drive the number of actual disk blocks which have been read for swapping, or loading run time systems. For example, in the first sample period, numbered two, there were 13 read requests for swap of RSTS loads, whilst a total of 768 blocks were read in connection with those 13 requests. This averages out at nearly 60 blocks per request, representing about 15kw of memory, which just happens to be the size of many of the programs running at this sample time. The purely swapping statistics are shown under the "DPO:.SWAP.WRT.CNT" heading, which is the number of write requests received for swaps on DPO:, and the "DPO:SWAP.WRT.BLK" figures is the number of blocks written for swaps. A comparison of the read and write for swaps figures shows a very close correlation in most of the sample periods, illustrating once again the roll-in and roll-out nature of this kind of job swapping.

Turning now to Figure 7.7b, we shall examine the all-important CPU usage statistics. The column headed "%NULL.TICS" indicates the percentage of clock ticks during which no use could be found for the CPU. In all cases on the sample printout this was zero. This indicates that the system is either very CPU intensive, or that it is CPU inefficient.

In either case, if a rerun of QSTATS produces similar results, it could be confidently stated that the processor should be upgraded. Further, it could be stated that adding any further users will be futile, since it will slow down existing users considerably. Beside the "%NULL.TICS" column in the printout is the "%USER.TICS" column. The values here indicate the percentage of the time that users' jobs were still actually running (as opposed to waiting for some system response, user input or disk I/O to occur) at the end of their run-burst. If this is low – as in this case, averaging around 36 per cent – the runbursts of the user jobs could be reduced to good effect, since nearly two/thirds of user runbursts at present are partially wasted. By experimenting with the length of runbursts until the "%USER.TICS" average increases, the "tweeker" can determine just how much of the runburst can usefully be trimmed off.

The leftmost column is the "%SYS.UNCH.TICS". These figures represent the percentage of CPU time not charged to any user, but which was used by the RSTS monitor for its own work, providing monitor service to user jobs.

Moving to Figure 7.7c, we can see the file processor statistics. Taking these from left to right, the first column is the "%FIP.NEEDED" statistics. This represents percentage of the time that the file processor (FIP) had requests pending or executing. The next column shows the "%FIP.IDLE" times. These are the percentage of the time that FIP was not actually running. The "%FIP.WAITING" column shows the percentage of time that FIP was waiting for some other system component to complete some operation for it. The fourth column shows the percentage of the sample period during which FIP was waiting for some overlay code to be loaded. Finally, the "%FIP.DISK.WAIT" statistics shows the percentage of time spent waiting for disk transfers to complete. If the disk wait time is high, some attempt should be made to improve the file and directory cacheing arrangements, since if the file processors requirements can be met from cache, then the overall speed of file processing can be speeded.

Progressing to Figure 7.7d, more file processor statistics can be seen. The "%FIP.CPU" time figures are the percentage of time that FIP required the CPU.

Next comes the "%IO.TIME", which is the percentage of time that was spent in executing interrupt services routines. If spurious interrupts are occurring in short bursts, this figure will be very erratic during periods of inactivity.

Now the directory I/O statistics beginning in Figure 7.7e; we saw in chapter four how the system performance can be adversely affected by fragmented directories. Referring to the figure the column headed "DPO:DIR.R.PHY.CNT" is the figures for the number of read requests which were needed to access information requested by the file processor. "DPO:DIR.R.PHY.BLK" are the figures showing the number of disk blocks which were read to satisfy these requests. The amount of cross referencing between directory blocks (as discussed in chapter four) can be quantified approximately by comparing these two sets of figures, since if one read request were to generate, say, ten blocks being read, then it would be obvious that a good deal of cross referencing must be occurring. In the sample printout shown here the relationship is one to one, indicating a well-maintained and unfragmented structure. Finally, "DPO:DIR.R.CHE.CNT" in Figure 7.7f shows directory reads which were satisfied from the cache – avoiding actual disk accesses. Again, the figures in the samples shown here are good, with an average of eighty requests per sample being met in this way. Many of the other statistics presented by QSTATS are to do with the SATT file. The SATT is the Storage Allocation Table, a bit map of the disk clusters. If a bit is set, it indicates that the cluster is in use. If clear, then the cluster represented by the bit is unused. As disk space is requested or relinquished, this table must be modified. Consequently, the SATT access statistics are of interest, since it will be one of the most frequently accessed items of information on a RSTS disk. The SATT-related statistics obtained with the sample printout we have been examining through this chapter were all very good; consequently, there would be little to gain by reproducing them, since no problem areas existed to examine.

By using the enormous amount of information provided by the QSTATS program the system manager or system "Tweeker" can attain, by trial and error combined with intelligent guesswork, optimum RSTS performance.

7.5 Altering systems to make them run more efficiently.

System "tweeking", as it is often referred to, entails examining all the information available about system software and system hardware. After this information has been scrutinised the points where potential for improvement exists can usually be pinpointed. Inefficient system usage often stems from badly planned application planning. It may also be caused by ad hoc application expansion, where programs are expanded and users added without any real thought of how the overall system may be affected. Similarly, extra hardware may be added without any real research on the effect that its addition may have on the existing system. Prime examples of this include the addition of extra DMA devices where the existing DMA devices are taking up all the spare bus time. In such a situation adding another DMA device may tip the balance, resulting in greatly increased bus access wait times, slower disk transfer and consequent system slowdown. In summary, the sensible planning of applications packages, and their maintenance, along with caution in fitting new hardware devices, will help to prevent system saturation, before the real saturation point in a particular application development is reached.

As an example of how the application software can make or break system efficiency, we shall look now at the mechanics of job swapping. This subject will be examined in detail here, as we shall shortly see how excessive swapping can be avoided by careful program design.

When a whole user job area must be swapped out of memory into a swap – (or checkpoint-) file, a number of things must take place before the actual roll-in and roll-out process can begin. Swapfiles are usually partitioned into slots. This arrangement will lead to the layout as shown in Figure 7.8. This shows a swapfile partitioned into three sections, A, B and C. Real swapfiles usually contain many more sections. Each section of our file – called a "swap slot" – will be large enough to contain a user job of the largest permissable size, as defined by the system manager. The small control section "X" shown may or may not exist, but if it does it will show the status of each swap slot. The status will show if the slot is occupied or unoccupied, and optionally some information about the user job contained in it, if occupied. When the need for a user job swap is detected, the operating system swapper must find a spare swap slot in the swapfile, or it must find the slot which contains the user job which it wants to roll-in to memory to replace the space which is currently occupied by the job it is going to roll-out. Once this is done the next phase involves an assessment of any better alternative part of memory into which the user job being rolled-in will fit. If careful placing of user jobs in memory is employed the fragmentation of available memory can be avoided.
(This, of course, will be avoided where memory management hardware is in use.) Finally the swap is executed, and the newly re-loaded user's job will in due course have a burst of processor usage. If a moment's thought is given to this process, it should be readily apparent that the odd swap of a job will not adversely affect system performance. The "perceived speed" factor mentioned earlier in the

text will suffer greatly however, when every user has to be swapped in or out prior to every runburst.

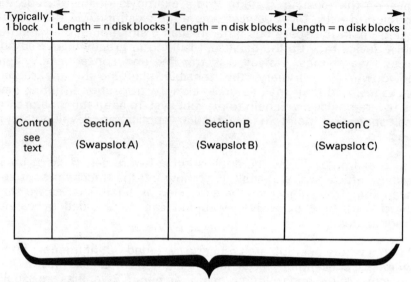

Simple swapfile. Three swap slots for swapping three users into or out of, as required. Each slot must be large enough to hold a user job of the maximum allowable size.

Figure 7.8   Simple swapfile layout

A simple example may prove to illustrate how system performance can be crippled by swapping. Imagine that two user jobs must be swapped. Job A is ready to run, but swapped out. Job B has just had a runburst of CPU time, during which it requested keyboard input; this may take some few seconds, so the job scheduler has decided to swap job A out to disk. The steps described above are taken, and the two jobs will be swapped over with no change in memory location, or swap slot. To take a typical case we will assume that each of the two jobs is 14kw in size.

Given that the size of a disk block is 1/2KB, we can easily calculate that there will have to be 56 blocks written, and 56 blocks read to carry out the swap. (14KW = 28KB = 56 1/2KB blocks) For a cartridge drive the average time to read or write a single block is something like two milliseconds. Ignoring for now all the overheads, which will be variable, writing then reading 56 blocks will take (very approximately) 220 milliseconds. This is of course an optimum figure for the stated specifications. Now, what about those overheads? If we add on a couple of the overheads we have up to now ignored, the reasons for avoiding wholesale user job swapping becomes abudantly clear.

When a disk drive has to move its read/write heads from one position to another, the operation (called a seek) will obviously take a finite time to carry out. For an average cartridge disk drive the quoted average seek time is around 45 milliseconds. Imagine a cartridge disk rotating at 2400 revolutions per minute. The read/write heads are seeking to the commanded track (or cylinder) in order to read a sector (we shall call it sector three). Just as the heads finish their travel the middle of sector three is under them. For obvious reasons the sector can only be read from its beginning. Due to this, the read can only begin when the disk has completed the best part of a complete revolution which, in the case of a 2400 r.p.m., disk will take around 25 milliseconds.

This is called rotational latency. The average rotational latency depends to a large extent on the rotational speed of the disk; the faster the rotation, the shorter the average latency. For our cartridge drive an average latency would be around 12 milliseconds. If we add to our original read and write time of 220 milliseconds two lots of latency times, plus one seek time, we get:

```
220 ms = (read and write combined)
 24 ms = (two average latency times)
 45 ms = (average seek time)
 ───────
289 ms      for a swap
 ───────
```

So our final figure (ignoring processor time in setting up the transfer) is 289 milliseconds for the complete swap. Considering that the user job may only get a burst of CPU time lasting 50ms, it is easy to see that the system may spend more time effecting swaps than doing the actual progressing of user jobs! This swapping time can of course be reduced by utilising higher performance disk units. The faster the rotation, and the shorter the average seek time of a disk drive, the shorter time a swap will take. Even with the best disk units, wholesale user job swapping must still be avoided at all costs. Avoiding swapping is done by the combination of buying enough memory to accomodate all foreseeable users, and careful planning of applications software. Planning applications software with overall system efficiency in mind will now be discussed.

In an average commercial environment the user is presented, when he logs into the system, with a "menu". This consists of a list of options from which he may choose one. The "menu" is printed up by one program, a fresh program will be loaded to implement the option he chooses, and then the menu program is reloaded to present the options again when the current function is fulfilled. This is illustrated in Figure 7.9. This loading and reloading of programs might seem a little I/O intensive, but if the sizes of the individual programs are kept small, by means of strict modularisation of the programs, the total eradication of swapping can be achieved. This is especially true where a single copy of a program in memory can be shared by many users, rather than needing a fresh copy of the program for every user running it. Keeping the software modular presupposes that there exists on the system a method of passing data between programs, so that data input to one program may be stored into data files by another. Every system must allow that this data forwarding be done via temporary disk files, but this method will add to the disk I/O required. A number of systems allow programs to pass a limited amount of data on to the programs to which they pass control, usually via a system call. Careful design of the application software, to keep its size down and ensure that its implementation uses the most efficient methods available, will speed the useful throughput of all systems. System specific examples will not be given here, but most of the currently available operating systems have section(s) in their manual sets on which are the most efficient methods to use when writing applications software.

As to altering hardware to make a given system run more effectively, it is important to find out if one particular subsystem (disk, memory or interfaces) is the weakest link, or if the processor itself is insufficient for the usage it is being given. A little time spent on assessment of what is required is better than a lot of money spent on a hardware upgrade which results in a disappointing performance improvement. Before spending vast amounts of money on faster hardware, the possibility that inefficient applications software could be tidied up should first be examined. When a partial upgrade is all that can be afforded it is imperative that system statistics be examined, in conjunction with expert advice, before taking the plunge. Software rewriting is expensive, but although faster hardware may increase the throughput of any software package, inefficient software will always deny achieving the full potential of any machine on which it is running. (The foregoing comments assume that upgrades to processors are software-compatible – as in the case of the PDP-11, and VAX range.) As a more specific example of how more sophisticated hardware can assist any CPU in the execution of its job we will now look at the alternatives to the basic "Simple" terminal interface device.

It can be readily appreciated that when there are a number of terminals attached to a computer system, each with a user typing commands or data at the keyboard, then the number of interrupts generated by the terminal interfacing electronics will be high. The most basic type of interface (for the purposes of this discussion we shall refer to these as "Simple" terminal interfaces) does not have any internal buffers except a received character register and a transmit character register. If the CPU does not respond to the interrupt generated by the reception of a character from a keyboard before another is received, the first character will be lost. Far more of a problem than characters typed into a computer, from the point of view of the number of interrupts, is the number of interrupts generated by completion of outputting a character.

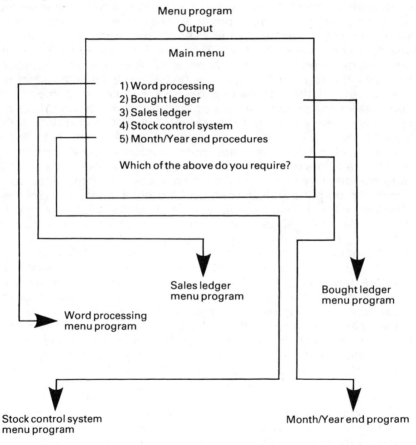

The program which prints up the main menu, and obtains input from the user as to which sub system he wishes to use, represents the entry point in a 'menu driven' system. If all the sub menu programs, and the implementation programs are kept modular and small then considerable benefit will result – see text.

Figure 7.9 Menu system overview

A moment's reflection on the nature of use of a terminal will make it apparent that the number of characters output is guaranteed to exceed the number input in just about every case. For example, on a VMS system merely to type the seven characters "SHO DEV" will produce a whole screen full of device details. This is the case for most system commands: a very few characters input will result in the output of a great many. In the case study of system statistics earlier in this chapter we saw that in a ten second sample over 4,000 characters were output to the system terminals. This is an extreme case, but illustrates the size to which the problem can grow. The procedure involved in interrupt servicing varies between machines, but generally the character input or output routines will take longer to set up than to execute. In the PDP-11, for example, the terminal interface will raise an interrupt. When no higher priority interrupt is asserted the interface will be allowed a bus access. Next, the interface sends its interrupt vector out on the bus. (The vector is the address of the address of the interrupting device's handler in memory.) The contents of the vecotr address passed out from the interface now contents of the vector address passed out from the interface now become the new contents of the program counter, with the previous executing at the address containing the interrupt service routine, in this case a terminal driver. When the system outputs a character the terminal driver will take the next character from the interrupting terminal's output buffer in memory and place it into the terminal's interface output register – or punch buffer, as the DEC convention has it. Then the terminal driver will exit. Only in the case of some other processing being required, like for example, setting a flag to show that the output buffer is now empty, will the overall time taken to transfer the single character be appreciably greater than the time it took to get into the terminal driver. This "interrupt overhead" problem has resulted in the development of terminal interfaces with extended capabilities, relieving the CPU of some or all of the responsibility for single character transfers. When massive amounts of characters are moved from system to terminals – as in the case of a data base or word processing application - a worthwhile improvement in system performance will be gained. Let us now examine how this is achieved. Interfaces which provide more than the basic functions for terminal to processor communication are variously called, "Terminal multiplexers" (abbreviated to terminal mux) or "Communications controllers", abbreviated to Comms controllers. Along with the variation in names comes a wide range of facilities offered. These include character recognition, MODEM support, synchronous and asycronous modes, auto echo and internal self test. Many manufacturers are now producing this type of hardware – much of it directly hardware-compatible with existing major manufactures' machines.

The most commonly found features, those which provide the basic reasons for replacing "Simple" interfaces with a terminal mux, will now be examined.

As a single-sentence raison d'etre for a terminal mux, it can be said that it enables system software to treat terminal I/O in a similar way to block device I/O, with a corresponding reduction in CPU supervision. This is substantially true, with the reservation that the blocks of data involved will be rather smaller than those used in disk or tape transfers. The typical terminal mux utilises a microprocessor - or similar large logic building block – along with support logic and electronics, to implement a complete terminal I/O control subsystem. The number of terminal lines serviced by such a subsystem may be up to 64 lines, and will probably be at least eight lines even in a minimum form.

In the general case output to the terminals attached to a terminal mux will proceed in the following steps. First, the terminal's output buffer in the computer memory is filled with characters to be output, either by the system or from a user program. Second, the control registers for the terminal mux are programmed to contain the address in the computer's memory where the terminal's output buffer exists, and the number of characters to be fetched from it and output, also the number of the terminal channel to which the characters are to be output. The CPU involvement now ceases until the fourth step. The third step is that the terminal mux now proceeds to fetch each character from the computer memory, using its Direct Memory Access (DMA – see glossary) capability. In some types of mux the whole buffer may be read into some internal SILO or memory on the mux itself at one go, effecting a true block transfer; whilst in others the characters are transferred one by one. With every character sent to the terminal line the character count is decremented by one, and when all the data has been sent out to the terminal the mux generates an interrupt to the CPU. Fourth, the interrupt from the mux causes either the refilling of the output buffer with yet more characters ready for output, or the output sequence termination, if there are no more to be output.

In the above example, the "interrupt overhead" is minimal. If, for example, 32 characters are to be transferred per sequence, the number of interrupts generated by a "simple" interface will be 32. Using the terminal mux method the number of interrupts will be only one (when the mux has transferred all the characters). A similar saving will result in the case of inputting characters via a terminal mux. The actual methods used to input characters from terminals to a system via a mux are less easy to generalise about. This is because the details depend on the level of intelligence of the mux. If, for example, the mux is able to recognise characters like DEL and input terminators, then processor involvement can be absolutely minimal, with the terminal input being echoed, and first-level parsed by the mux. If the mux possesses the auto echo facility but not the character examination facility the processor will have to examine the input buffer in its memory regularly, in order to search for an input terminator, or other character which it must respond to immediately. (A DEC example of such a character is Control/C.) Even in the case where the terminal mux has only the minimum extras needed to distinguish it from a "simple" interface, the DMA feature inherent in the device will almost completely remove the "interrupt overhead" which makes the "simple" interface so processor intensive. Let us now look at an input sequence for a terminal connected to a terminal mux with auto echo but no character assessing facility. First, the user at the terminal types in a character. Second, the terminal mux receives the character and echoes it back to the terminal (control characters are not echoed by most muxes). Third, the terminal mux now performs a DMA to the computer memory, placing the character in the area of memory designated by the system software as the terminal's input buffer. Fourth, the terminal driver examines the input buffer for a line terminator or character which must be actioned immediately. If none is found, then the cycle begins again. If a character is found which needs immediate actioning, the action is carried out. Once again, the processor involvement does not include the "interrupt overhead" — and at normal processor speeds the input buffer scanning need only be relatively infrequent. As already stated, the average system will have a great deal more character output than input occurring.

Consequently, the greater efficiency of character output using a terminal mux will benefit almost all applications, but most especially those like data bases, word processing or program development.

From a purely hardware standpoint the disadvantages of using the terminal mux approach described above apply only when malfunctions occur. If the microprocessor on board the terminal mux crashes, as it certainly will for anything more than the most simple failures, the end result is liable to be more serious for the system as a whole than a malfunction in a "simple" interface would be. This is because the mux has a DMA capability. Often when a microprocessor crashes it goes into a "runaway" state, executing random, and totally unintended, sequences of instructions. The outcome of this is very often bus grabbing without regard to bus arbitration signals, or hanging up interrupt lines, etc., thus causing the whole system to crash! These problems should not deter one from purchasing a terminal mux, since they will occur only very, very rarely with reputable makes.

Completely separate from any software considerations are good hardware maintenance procedures. In general it is better to spend more on a maintenance contract with a service company which specialises in your particular machine type, since they will be more likely to have a ready stock of bits for your machine, and the engineers will be more likely to know about it. If good hardware maintenance procedures are followed, faults which slow down devices actually causing the operating system to log errors on them can be avoided. This slow device problem is often the result of badly adjusted servo systems on printers and disk devices, causing them to perform operations below their optimum speeds. The adjustments referred to should be made if a unit seems to be slow, or perhaps annually. Another hardware area which can be detrimental to system performance is media. Disks should be regularly checked for surface damage, and their recording surfaces cleaned. If disk condition is allowed to deteriorate disk retries, as discussed in chapter six, can occur repeatedly, slowing disk subsystem throughput, and some disk units may only take longer to perform an operation without logging an error. Likewise, magnetic tape media should be replaced when worn. If many retries to write data to tape have to be performed, then once again a significant increase in time spent on tape jobs will occur. This will be especially annoying where the system tape units form the backup medium for Winchester technology disk units. Media maintenance should be performed by specialist companies. Media purchased should be of a reputable make, and be the best which can be afforded. Cost cutting at the time of media purchase can easily result in problems at a later stage.

7.6. System alterations: other considerations

Finally, on the subject of altering system parameters and hardware to obtain better performance from a given configuration, let us look at the pitfalls.

When more DMA interfaces are added to a system there is a danger that the non-DMA devices remaining may have a tough time getting bus access, resulting in lost data. Sometimes the only really accurate way of finding out if this is going to happen is to actually add the hardware on a trial basis and see if any problems of this nature occur.

On paper adding more hardware may leave the existing power supplies with some spare capacity, but bear in mind that power supply maximum ratings may only be stress (or absolute maximum) ratings, and the power supply system may not take a continuous load at the new rating for the rest of the machine's lifetime.

When you alter the relative priorities of the users on the system, keep it clearly in mind that those users receiving better response times are doing so at the expense of the lower priority users remaining. Ensure that only those users with important terminal interactive jobs get a higher priority level.

Where applicable, ensure that hardware priority levels are set to the correct levels. In a machine like the PDP-11, where some interfaces have variable priority levels and hardware adjustable transfer burst levels, use trial and error to ensure that the settings are correct for the particular configuration.

Read your terminal hardware manuals. Ensure that the terminal characteristics set up for your terminals are correct. If, for example, your terminals can action the TAB character correctly, by moving the cursor forward eight positions, then make sure that the operating system knows this. If the operating system has a list of characteristics for your terminals which says that they cannot directly action a TAB, then it will output eight spaces instead, octupling the characters output. Again, examine and experiment with the number of null characters which are output to your VDUs and matrix printers after a carriage return (usually called FILL characters). If there are too many FILL characters, you are wasting time outputting those not required. The same can be said of the form feed and rubout characters.
Another small saving is to use half duplex, saving the CPU echoing any input characters. The importance of the terminal settings will be greatest when the system performs a lot of text editing and/or word processing, but might adversely affect systems where programs are being listed out to user terminals all the time. Reducing the output baud rate to terminals may also yield improvements to general throughput. It is often recommended that terminals be reduced from 9,600 baud to 2,400 baud transfer rate on RSTS systems, for example. The resulting reduction in the speed at which terminal output is produced is only minimal, but the rate at which interrupts are generated is significantly reduced. Try to ensure, by the careful monitoring of the system, that any changes made do not place undue demands on any particular part of the system. If, for example, you add a new disk drive to be run by an existing controller, and you use the disk as a home for rarely accessed files and as a swapping disk, you

may be creating a bottleneck. If this happens, there may be no benefit gained from the third drive, since the controller itself will be the limiting factor.

In conclusion, it can be said that with a combination of correct hardware and software maintenance in conjunction with careful monitoring of system performance, optimum system performance can be attained and kept. Additionally, this will ensure that when money becomes available to upgrade hardware the owner will know the most effective ways to spend it. Often an entire upgrade is not needed: faster disks or more memory will achieve the desired improvements. With a system run properly, the time when an entire upgrade will be needed will be more easily recognisable.

CHAPTER 8
"Getting Personal"

With the announcement, made some little time ago, that DEC had managed to produce on one VLSI (Very Large Scale Integration) chip a PDP-11/70 processor, the way to the future was pointed. The announcement was greeted with cries which varied from "I don't believe it!" to "About time, too". In the market place the end manifestation of this spectacular development is the LSI-11/73. This consists of a single board which is functionally equivalent to an 11/70 or a 11/44. It can support up to 4mb of memory, located on separate boards. This 4mb includes cache. By comparison, the PDP-11/70 — constructed from discrete logic building blocks, consists of up to 18 boards, each of which is three times the size of the 11/73 boards. The 11/70 additionally needs large arrays of cooling fans, and a set of hefty power supplies.

The entire PDP-11 concept is in for a drastic repackaging. With the production of VLSI chips to replace what was previously contained on several boards, the physical size of each of the PDP-11 processors can be greatly reduced. This will allow the remarketing of the PDP-11 range as the 1100 series. When Mr. Average comes home from his day at the office in ten years time, he might well sit down to play PAC-MAN on his home micro, which functions identically to — but looks nothing like - today's PDP-11/44 or PDP-11/70. It will be very interesting to see how the operating systems for these new "super microcomputers" are derived. Will the current ones be transferred? In theory, they easily could be, since the new machines will be software-compatible. Perhaps more likely is that new or subset operating systems will be used. There does not seem much point in carrying out a straight transfer of a multi-user operating system which can run perhaps forty users, when the machine you are putting it on to is going to be sold as a small business or home computer. Besides this, the features desirable in a multi-user operating system are not necessarily those which will sell the machine to buyers of small personal operating systems. The differences which exist between multi-user operating systems like VMS, RSX and RSTS, which run in commercial or institutional environments, when compared with single user versions of CP/M and its derivatives, make the operating systems which will run on the VLSI versions of today's minicomputers rather difficult to predict. The most likely outcome will be a kind of distillation of those facilities of each which will be of most use to personal computer users.

At the moment, DEC have two products out on sale which are specifically aimed at the personal computer market. These are the Rainbow 100 range and the Professional 300 series. The operating systems for these two systems are different, and accordingly will be examined separately.

The Rainbow 100 series uses that most popular of personal computer operating systems, CP/M, in a combinational version called CP/M-86/80. In addition, the Rainbow can also support Microsoft's very popular MSDOS operating system. With the choice of two operating systems available, the Rainbow is an attractive choice to commercial users who want to ensure the widest possible choice of off-the-shelf software packages. Further, as the operating system is loaded from disk into the Rainbow after each power-on, the owner can purchase both operating systems, which can be run in turn according to requirements. This will greatly increase the amount of ready-to-run software available.

In hardware terms the Rainbow consists of up to four floppy disk units, (total disk capacity of 1.6mb), a keyboard and video monitor subsystem and a dual processor configuration consisting of a Zilog Z80 microprocessor and an Intel 8088. The basic machine has 64kb of RAM, which can be upgraded. In addition, there are 24kb of ROM-based firmware containing self-test diagnostics, and various emulation, bootstrap, initialisation and service routines. Only one interactive terminal plus one printer can be utilised on the Rainbow, thus making it very definitely a personal computer.

The Rainbow will run either 16-bit or eight-bit CP/M or CP/M 86-based programs, and can automatically recognise them and have the correct processor execute them. This feature is further enhanced by the support of system calls for both CP/M 80 and CP/M 86. CP/M is a very well-documented operating system, and the reader is referred to the many good books available on it for more details of its features and capabilities. MSDOS is claimed to be the most widely used disk operating system for personal computers based on Intel's 8088 and 8086 microprocessors. It was designed to run as fast and efficiently as possible, and to have total compatibility with CP/M 80 translated programs. To achieve the speed and efficiency the file structure was designed for speed above everything else, and the original MSDOS was written in assembly language, for a Z80. The major components of MSDOS are the I/O handler, which is a device-independent I/O control module, the command processor which interprets and actions the command entered by the user, and the I/O system, which is a totally device-dependent device driver system. The command processor is split into two sections, one of which is only loaded into memory when needed. This minimises the space it takes up. There are tree structured directories available on some versions of MSDOS, whilst other versions have only a single level directory. With its wide usage MSDOS Rainbow users have a good choice of software application packages available off the shelf.

DEC's other entrant in the personal computer race is the Professional 300 series. At the heart of the Professional system is the PDP11/23 equivalent F11 processor. From a software point of view the F11 is practically identical to the 11/23. The only difference in programming the 11/23 and the F11 is that on the Professional system the I/O addresses are different from those used on the full size 11/23. This is due to each 'Option slot' having a dedicated address for I/O, and during power up each slot is interrogated to see what device is plugged in to it. This means that a minimal amount of changes to transmigrated software is needed. A package of software is available to do this and much more (see next paragraph). The system bus on the Professional is not the QBUS used on the PDP11/23 system. The Professional uses its own bus, called the CTI bus, which, like the Qbus, multiplexes address and data. The F11 can address up to 4 mb of memory using a memory management unit (MMU). As a standard the Professional comes with ½mb of memory and a floating point adaptor. Other important hardware features are: one interactive terminal, consisting of a detachable keyboard and a monitor (Black and white or colour), and the system unit containing the floppy disc unit(s). The Professional 350 can house internally a 10mb winchester technology disk unit greatly increasing the speed and storage capacity over the 325 which uses 5.25inch 800kb floppy disk units. A serial printer and communications ports are standard on the 325 and the 350, with real time interface option providing two more as an optional extra.

The software side of the Professional is, as one would expect on a machine with 90 per cent of the throughput of its minicomputer relation, impressively powerful. Using the P/OS operating system, which is derived from RSX11M as its basis, the machine can support multitasking, with all but the task actually being interacted with on the system terminal being placed in the background. P/OS can run up to a maximum of 31 tasks, using the latest version of P/OS - V1.7, depending on their size and make-up. For tasks which are not interactive to any significant degree, being in the background is no great problem, since they merely complete their processing and then await the terminal user's attention. Highly interactive tasks might be more of a problem. P/OS is defined by DEC as a "multi-tasking real time resource-sharing system", and its file structure protocol is identical to that used on PDP-11 and VAX systems. Purchasers of the Professional can also get an additional "tool kit" software package. This greatly extends the machine's capabilities with, for instance, a program being included to see all the current background tasks, their states and general system information. This program = "RMD" – is very like the RSX program of the same name, see fig. 8.1. Also included in the package is software to convert existing PDP-11 software to run on the Professional. (Incidentally, there is also a version of the conversion software to run on PDP-11 or VAX processors, which generates Professional-compatible code on to a transfer media or an interconnecting RS232 line for installation into the Professional). As well as all this the "tool kit" package contains a PIP (Peripheral Interchange Program) and a few other odds and ends. The Text editor "PROSE" comes as standard with every Professional system, and this makes the machine useful for office applications, as well as number crunching or data processing. P/OS version 1.7 is the latest available at the time of writing, and due to improved screen write techniques and generally better internal organisation is reckoned to be rather faster than its predecessor, version 1.5. The DEC EDT text editor is also now available to run inder P/OS V1.7. For those people used to PDP's or VAX operating systems, there are a number of DEC standards in evidence. A subset of DCL (Digital Command Language) is used and you can use some control characters as you would on PDP's or VAX's: for example, you can use CTRL/C to exit from programs under some circumstances.

The amount of the system memory used by P/OS varies, as it makes extensive use of overlays once the amount of free memory becomes low. At its full size, P/OS is about 256kb, but if the user tasks expand to take up all the rest of the memory, and then require more, P/OS contracts its size by offloading those modules of itself which it can run without, and which can be called in as overlays if they are required. This makes the amount of available memory to user tasks variable, and adds great flexibility to the machine. It does have the effect that if P/OS has to greatly contract itself it would run more slowly when an appreciable number of overlays must be loaded to service tasks. For machine users who do not want to learn yet another set of commands

```
RSX-11M-PLUS V2 BL18.0 (PRO350)  256K   UP 000:00:01      17-OCT-91 09:48:24
TASK= TFW...                     FREE=   SY0:10615.  DZ1:DMO
                                         DW2:OFL      DZ2:DMO                  PARS
POOL=4870.:5138.:27.            SECPOOL=102.:128.:79%
     4870.:5138.:27.                    102.:128.:79%                   SECPOL:P
                                                                        DRVPAR:D
IN:        D T T D  V    $    $   F  VR RR RRRR P T I S C      P  P      TFWCOM:D
10         Z T F I  D    G    V   1  EM MM MMMM O F N U O      O  R      BITMAP:D
52K        : : W R  F    I    T   1  RS SS SSSS S W S M M      S  E      CVDATA:D
OUT:       . 1 N    D    1    A   .R LL LLLL S . R L M         R  T      GEN   :D
0          . 1 · T  I    0    C   .E BB BBBB U . E O G         E  C      CNFTBL:D
OK         . M  S   S    2    P   .S AB CDEF M . M G R         S  L      IO PAR:D
           )==)-+=!==!=====!=!====>>=!!=!!!!=!!==>=JJ--> !---!-
0********16******32******48******64******80******96******112*****
E---P-----P-D--D-D-----------------------------------------------------
----------------------------------------------------------------------D
128*****144*****160*****176*****192*****208*****224*****240*****
> <-->      !--!                                  <>====>==>
     R       S                                    X  C  C     ERRSEQ
     M       E                                    K  $  $     0.
     D       R                                    M     C
     T       S                                    A     T
     1       A                                    I     E
             P                                    N     X
```

Figure 8.1

P/OS has a full menu driven environment available as standard. In a menu driven environment, instead of having to remember the exact command or sequence of commands which must be typed in to the machine to do a specific job, a menu or list of available system functions is presented, from which you choose one that you want. Your choice then takes you into a submenu, which will offer you all the specific operations of that type of function. For example, if from the main menu you choose Disk/Diskette services, you then go into a submenu on which all the disk related operations are offered, COPY, INITIALISE, etc. Many people most especially beginners or people who are not computer oriented find this type of command giving easier than memorising command sequences. The concept of personal computers based on highly compressed versions of existing minicomputers is very challenging, nowhere more so than in creating operating systems which take full advantage of the compatibility with existing software, yet offer the right mix of facilities and human interface qualities which personal computers' users need. The personal computer owner is far less likely to be a computer professional than his minicomputer counterpart, and allowance has to be made for this in creating an environment in which personal computers can justify their existence. This must be done without choking off purchasers' enthusiasm by over-complex operating procedures, and tidal waves of what people newly introduced to computers see as gobbledegook, but which computer professionals regard as justifiable jargon!

I must confess that in writing this book I have been amazed at the difficulty of expressing some computer concepts without resorting to jargon, and on some occasions had to defer this problem till I came to write the glossary! Nevertheless, I hope that the book has shed light on somebody's darkness, and that the reader feels able to look at a DEC operating system with more confidence than before reading it. Future trends in operating systems are of course difficult to predict. It is almost certain, however, that as memory gets cheaper and therefore more plentiful, the "keep it small" approach of days gone by will disappear, and that as system hardware becomes more complex, though more compact, the hardware management aspects of operating systems will be delegated to peripheral processors. Whatever happens, I am sure the subject will remain an interesting one.

APPENDIX 1
Useful Information

Here are a couple of programs which readers can use for helping in crash dumps or other informational dumps. The first is a program to convert Octal numbers into their decimal equivalents. The second, which will only work on VDU's featuring direct cursor addressing in this format, (this was for a Systime 5762), positions the cursor on screen at the chosen co-ordinates. Both programs are written for use on PDP-11's or VAX's with BASIC-PLUS or BASIC-PLUS 2 available, though other BASIC's will probably take them too.

```
500 !   OCTAL TO DECIMAL CONVERTER PROGRAM.
        LINES 500,1000,4010,4020 AND 5200 ARE OPTIONAL AND MAY BE LEFT
        OUT FOR A QUICK VERSION.

1000 Print "Octal TO decimal converter"
2000 Input "What is your octal number";Z$
3000 P=1        : T=0
4000 For I%= len(Z$) to 1% step -1%
4005     X$=MID(Z$,I%,1%)
4010     IF VAL(X$) < 8% THEN GOTO 4100
4020     PRINT X$ " is out of range for an octal number" : Goto 2000
4100     T=T+(VAL(X$)*P)
4200     P=P*8
5000 Next I%
5100 Print Z$;" Octal = ";T;" Decimal"
5200 Goto 2000    !Run again if required
32767 End
```

For terminals featuring DIRECT CURSOR ADDRESSING only

```
27900 !
        A SUBROUTINE TO POSITION THE CURSOR AT THE COORDINATES SET BY
        THE RECIEVED VARIABLES X% AND Y% XX=COL AND YX=ROW
            WE DO A CR (CHR$(13) FIRST SO THAT RSTS DOES NOT KEEP
        INSERTING L/F/ C/R PAIRS INTO THE LINE WHEN WE DONT WANT IT TO
        I.E. WE RESET POS(0) TO VALUE OF ZERO.

27910 PRINT CHR$(13%);CHR$(30%);CHR$(31+X%);CHR$(31+Y%);
27920 RETURN
```

CTRL	Decimal	Hex	Octal	Name	SIGNIFICANCES		
					RSX	**VMS**	**RSTS**
●	0	00	00	NULL	Fill character	Fill character	Fill character
A	1	01	01	SOH	none	none	none
B	2	02	02	STX	none	none	none
C	3	03	03	ETX	Place current task in background and return to MCR	Terminate current process, return to $ command level	Terminate current process, return to ready command level
D	4	04	04	EOT	none	none	none
E	5	05	05	ENQ	none	none	none
F	6	06	06	ACK	none	none	none
G	7	07	07	BEL	none	none	none
H	8	08	10	BS	none	none	none
I	9	09	11	HTAB	Tab character	Tab character	Tab character
J	10	0A	12	LF		Alternative input terminator	Input terminator
K	11	0B	13	VT	none	none	none
L	12	0C	14	FF	none	none	none
M	13	0D	15	CR	Carriage return input terminator	Input terminator	Input terminator
N	14	0E	16	SO	none	none	none
O	15	0F	17	SI	Suppress (Discard) terminal output until next ctrl O	Discard terminal output until next ctrl O	Discard terminal output until next ctrl O
P	16	10	20	DLE	none	None unless console terminal on VAX M/C	none
Q	17	11	21	DC1	Resume terminal output	Resume terminal output	Resume terminal output
R	18	12	22	DC2	Print out keyboard buffer contents	Print out keyboard buffer contents	Print out keyboard buffer contents
S	19	13	23	DC3	Stall terminal output	Stall terminal output	Stall terminal output
T	20	14	24	DC4		Show one line status report	Show one line status report
U	21	15	25	NAK	Clear input buffer out	Clear input buffer out	Clear input buffer out
V	22	16	26	SYN	none	none	none
W	23	17	27	ETB	none	none	none
X	24	18	30	CAN	none	As for NAK	none
Y	25	19	31	EM	none	As for ETX	none
Z	26	1A	32	SUB	Exit program at next prompt	Exit program at next prompt	Exit program at next prompt
●	27	1B	33	ESC	none	none	none
●	28	1C	34	FS	none	none	none
●	29	1D	35	GS	none	none	none
●	30	1E	36	RS	none	none	none
●	31	1F	37	US	none	none	none

● Varies according to terminal make

CTRL — The Control key and letter shown are pressed simultaneously to generate these codes

Name = ASCII name for character

ASCII control codes & significance to RSX, VMS & RSTS

149

APPENDIX TWO
RSTS Special
Features

Special features available from RSTS are a unique user friendliness. This applies nowhere more than in the error messages issued by RSTS. These are not so detailed that they become tedious, nor are they so abbreviated that they are not readily understood by inexperienced users.

Other features include the ability to completely detach (or place in the background) a job, either by use of the "CCONT" command, or under user program control, or the "/DET" switch on usage of a command. Unlike RSX, where it is not possible to be sure that the task will not reappear, or VMS, where there has to be input and log files to spawn a process, RSTS allows the detached job to continue until input or output is required. As a purely personal comment, I have found RSTS to be the most secure of the three operating systems, being able to carry on against unexpected hardware occurences, and also supplying information about them. This may be because, whilst RSTS is undoubtedly more reliable than RSX, VMS has a far more complex hardware configuration to cope with, and the overall system complexity of a VAX machine is greater than all but the largest standard PDP-11 processors. The concise command language system used under RSTS is not unique in its concept, but neither of the other two systems implement the feature in the same way. The Concise Command Language allows predefinition of an abbreviated version of a program name. During the execution of the start command file the system utility program "UTILTY" is used to perform this definition. Thereafter, all that is needed to run a program for which a CCL has been defined is to type the minimum specified command abbreviation for it. An example of this on almost every RSTS system is the "SY" command, which is nearly always installed as a CCL for "SYSTAT". This feature facilitates easy running of the programs used over and over again during the course of an average day's work on the computer.

RSX Special Features

RSX special features include the ability to place the current task in the background while another is started. This can be an extremely useful thing to do where, for example, there are no terminals spare, or where several different tasks must be monitored from one terminal. As with the other two operating systems the Digital Command Language is available on the latest version, which allows users to transfer between machines running any of the other two, with a reduced adaptation period.

On-line help messages are available to users, giving them the list of available commands and the uses to which they may be put. This help facility is available to users, whether they are logged on or not. RSX is best suited to scientific and control applications, at which it is best. The current versions of RSX are the most user friendly ever, and are a great improvement on previous versions in this respect. RSX allows abbreviations of its keyboard commands — usually to three letters - unless this would not completely identify the command.

VMS Special Features

VMS, like RSX, allows abbreviation of its commands, often to two letters. For example, the "SHOW WORKING_SET" command can be abbreviated to "SH W", which makes system work far easier and faster to perform.

Once again, DCL is available as the input interpreter, and whole programs may be written in DCL in the form of command files. The enormous amount of system performance information available from VMS utilities make it a very easy matter to find out how the system as a whole is performing. (Interpretation of these super-detailed statistics is another matter.) VMS possesses the "AUTOGEN" facility, which acts like an on-site expert. Autogen regenerates the VMS system parameters, with special regard to the particular machine on which it is running. The "SYSGEN" facility can be made to do very useful things like list out hardware, show system tables, symbols or names. The "DUMP" command can be used to show the contents of files held on the system in various output formats. The devices for which the system is configured can be changed online. The online help messages which are available to logged on users are both comprehensive and fast to call up.

Personally I find the complexity of the error messages issued by VMS for even silly mistakes a little excessive; in the case of error messages relating to more complex misdemeanours, however, I concede that the information they provide is sometimes useful.

151

APPENDIX THREE
SYSGENS

A "SYSGEN" is a procedure which assembles from a library of system modules those required to make a new image of an operating system for a specific machine. The purpose of performing a SYSGEN after a system has been installed and running, is to allow some new hardware item to be used on the system or to redefine some fundamental system characteristic or parameter. The method of performing a "SYSGEN" varies a little from one operating system to another, but precise details will not be given here. The general way in which a SYSGEN works is to connect together into a single executable machine code image all the required operating system components, along with the requisite parameter tables, lists, etc., to provide the required facilities. To determine what the newly generated system will provide for, a long question and answer session is often performed. At the end of this a SYSGEN parameter file will have been created, and from this all the required system component modules will be submitted to a system build program, interacting with MACRO or other assembler, which will eventually produce a new file containing the newly SYSGEN-ed operating system image. With the exception of VMS, which has its own "AUTOGEN" facility and therefore can be discounted from most of the points in this discussion, SYSGENs take an appreciable amount of time to execute. Additionally, if a hard copy listing of the source versions of the system is requested, a lot of paper may be required! Therefore it is important to allot enough time to the purpose, rather than rush through it and find that something is missing that was required, after trying out the new system. Make sure that the hardware you have, or plan to buy in the foreseeable future is included in the hardware which the new SYSGEN will support. Ensure that, if in the question and answer session the addresses of the Control and Status Registers (CRSs) are requested, you enter them correctly. If you enter these wrongly the system may fail altogether. Make sure, by reading the relevant manuals beforehand, that you understand at least the broad meaning of each question you are asked. More important than anything else, make sure you know exactly what hardware resources – devices, disk sizes, controller addresses and memory size – you have present on the system you are generating the new operating system to run on. Finally, try to run the SYSGEN at a time when other users are not on the system, not because the SYSGEN process will interfere directly with them, but because the CPU time needed for a SYSGEN may slow other users down to an unacceptable degree.

APPENDIX FOUR
Bibliography

This appendix lists some books which I have found informative in my research for this book, and also in my more general reading on the PDP-11. But also included are some books which the reader may like to peruse for information applicable to the ideas outlined here. These books are not written by or for DEC. The principal source of information on DEC operating systems and hardware is of course DEC manuals. The reader should be able to obtain access to DEC manuals for a particular system directly from DEC, or from your own system manager, who should have a complete set of applicable manuals. Happy reading!

BIBLIOGRAPHY

"Software Interpreters for Microcomputers" by Thomas C McIntyre

Published by John Wiley & Sons Inc. 1978

This book contains a wealth of information on the techniques which may be used to implement high level language interpreters. BASIC is the language used in the bulk of the examples, and although the actual microprocessor which is used on the machine whose details are included in the book is now more or less obsolete, the actual thinking behind the concepts and ideas presented is still highly relevant to readers who may like to take a detailed look at how BASIC interpretation takes place. The overall points discussed in the book are for single-user microprocessor-based systems, but many of them are transferrable to multi-user minicomputers, particularly those which relate to execution speed and efficiency. The writer maintains an awareness that many readers are not oriented to higher mathematics, and the book, although not thought suitable for novices, is highly readable and easy to follow.

"Machine and Assembly Language Programming of the PDP-11" by Arthur Gill

Published by Prentice-Hall Inc. 1978

This book is a real goldmine for anybody with an interest in PDP-11 assembly language or machine code programming. The hardware characteristics of the machines are detailed, and many useful subroutines, some applicable to operating systems, are built up and explained. The PDP-11 instruction set is listed, demonstrated and discussed. Particularly good is the section explaining addressing modes. System, mathematical and hardware handling subroutines are shown, and the operation of the assembly language is demonstrated. A thoroughly useful book for all PDP-11 low level users.

"Minicomputer Systems. Organisation, Programming and Applications (PDP-11)" by Richard H Eckouse, JR & L Robert Morris.

Published by Prentice-HAll Inc. 1979

As its title suggests, this book is an all round look at minicomputer with particular reference to the DEC PDP-11. I personally found it a book to pick out the interesting bits from and discard the rest. This may be because I have no great mathematical abilities, and there is a fair amount of mathematical content. However, there are very good sections on I/O device drivers, with many examples of specific DEC devices. There is a whole chapter on operating systems, but unfortunately this only uses DEC's RT-11 in specific examples. Having said this, however, the chapter is worth reading, as its overall content is interesting and well presented. There is no mention of any of the three operating systems we have used in this book. The section on microprogramming and micromachine hardware is centred around the PDP-11/60 and takes the reader through elementary logic circuits to the implementation of the 11/60 instruction set. Interrupts, boolean algebra, interactive graphics processing, assemblers and data structures are all covered.

"Computer Operating Systems" by D W Barron

Published by Chapman and Hall. 1971 (reprinted 1973 and 1975)

Many of the hardware details of this book are now very dated and, as usual, based on IBM and ICL practises. However, I have included it in this list because of the excellent section on filing systems, which is concise and clear. The reader will find that some parts of other sections may be of use.

"Operating Systems" by Madnick & Donovan

Published by McGraw Hill. 1981

Here is another book which uses IBM throughout in its application examples. The very long section on memory management is, in parts, excellent. But the whole book I found to be rather hard work, partly because of the advanced nature of some of the material, partly because of the mathematical approach used, and principally because of the alien nature of some of the hardware described. (Card readers and drums?) With these reservations I can recommend the general content of the device management chapter of the book. Each chapter ends with a set of questions which you may use to test your understanding of what you have just read.

GLOSSARY OF TERMS

ASCII

Short for American Standard Code for Information Interchange. An internationally accepted character code set, where each character of the alphabet, numbers, punctuation marks, symbols and control codes are represented by a known code, e.g. in ASCII the value 65 represents the letter "A".

BASIC

A programming language. DEC BASIC-PLUS is a super-set of the original BASIC.

BAUDS

The rate at which data is sent down a serial line. A standard set of BAUD rates are used in the computer industry. These usually start at 50 BAUD and go up to 39.2K BAUD. As a rule of thumb, a BAUD can be thought of as being equivalent to one bit per second.

BUS

A set of signal wires to which are connected the CPU, the computer memory and all the peripheral controllers and interfaces. Only one of these may use the BUS at one time, though that one will be taking some data out of, or putting data into, another of them.

CHECKSUM

As applied to disk data checking, a checksum is the value obtained by adding together all the bytes in a disk block. When reloading the block the typical disk controller recalculates what the checksum should be, and raises an error bit in its status register if the result is different from the checksum which it has just read. This system is not foolproof, for

157

if one byte drops a bit, while another raises that same bit, the checksum will still be good. For this reason several error detection techniques are used simultaneously on disks.

CLUSTER

A group of disk blocks which, for software purposes are treated as a single block, all blocks in the cluster being adjacent physically.

CONSOLE

As used in DEC circles means one of two things: 1) the master terminal attached to a system, which is the only one from which the system can be started or shut down, 2) the switches and lights on the front panel of some of the PDP-11s.

CONTIGUOUS

As applied to disk files, if a file is contiguous it is located in blocks on the disk which are adjacent to one another.

CPU

Abbreviation for Central Processing Unit. The part of the computer which performs the actual processing of data.

CPU BOUND

A CPU bound system has a CPU which cannot keep up with the demands upon it, leaving users requiring CPU time to wait for it.

CYLINDER

A cylinder is all the tracks on the surface of a disk which are at the same distance from the centre of the disk.

DATA BASE

A computer system on which a large amount of information is kept on line, so that it may be retrieved quickly and repeatedly. Data bases usually have users who rent time on the computer, or pay for information supplied from it: e.g. credit worthiness data bases.

DISK BOUND

A disk bound system has performance which is limited by the speed of its disk subsystem, with users queuing up for disk service.

DMA

Short for Direct Memory Access. This means that a device possessing DMA can directly read or write data into or out of the computer's memory without any help from the CPU.

EPROM

Short for Erasable Read Only Memory. Similar to a ROM (see ROM) but can be erased by some special means (like exposure to some kinds of ultra violet light). EPROMS can have their contents reprogrammed by anyone with the required simple machine to do it.

FILL CHARACTERS

These are used historically to allow for carriage return on old-style hard copy terminals. This works by outputting several Null (value zero) characters after every carriage return or line feed characters, to prevent characters being lost during the time the head is returning to the left hand margin. A few VDUs also need Fill characters to be sent after LF or CR characters; this is due to the possibility of "race" conditions occurring within the VDU.

FLOPPY DISK

A single platter diskette of fairly small size — one popular size, for example, is eight inches in diameter — the actual disk is flexible. The storage capacity of a floppy diskette varies according to the size, whether both surfaces are used for recording, and the recording method. Up to 3mbyte floppies exist, but the more common capacity is 1mbyte.

GIGO

Acronym for "garbage in, garbage out". In computing, as in other disciplines, the quality of your output will only be as good as your input. An Americanism.

GLITCH

In the sort of contexts covered by this book a glitch is one one-off hardware event which is not repeatable. The occurence of a glitch usually manifests itself by a unit or system failure which does not reoccur when the same operation is retried. Glitches are often due to mains dips or just to a temporary malfunction somewhere. The source of a true glitch is never traced!

HARD DISK

A single or multiple platter disk pack where the platters are rigid (made from steel or aluminium) covered in a very high precision coating of oxide on which the data is recorded. Capacities range from 5mbyte to 300mbyte and upwards.

HARDWARE

Anything to do with computers which either consumes electricity (e.g. boards) or houses something which does (e.g. a disk cabinet).

HEAD CRASH

On many hard disks the disk read/write heads float on a cushion of air built up by the rotating disk; this normally keeps them a few thousandths of an inch off the disk surface. If, however, some particle gets in between the heads and surface of the disk then the heads can plough into the surface, and usually the disk and the heads are damaged beyond repair – this is a head crash. Head crashes are expensive events, as disks are not cheap and disk heads can be very expensive.

INITIALISE

As applied to the action of initialising hardware within a computer: set all hardware elements of the computer to a known condition ready to start it. As applied to initialising media: creating data on the media which the computer operating system can read and recognise. This has to be done on new disks, for example.

I/O

Abbreviation for Input/Output. The I/O section of a computer's hardware will typically be any of the hardware remaining after the CPU itself and the memory and associated electronics are discounted.

MAGNETIC TAPE

Reel to reel tapes with up to nine tracks (eight data one parity). Often referred to by the abbreviation magtapes. These are sophisticated servo-controlled machines with control registers available to the host system. Usually DMA devices, they have nearly always got a complex controller which allows the software to program things like "write a block", "read a block" or "rewind to the beginning of the tape". Visually very satisfying.

MATRIX PRINTER

A printer whose printed characters are made up from a dot matrix, as opposed to type hammers.

MEDIA

The disks, tapes, paper tapes and even paper on which computer data is stored or printed.

MEDIA MAINTENANCE

Mostly applies to disks. Disks are checked at regular intervals to check on their state of wear and highlight any excessive wear.

OCTAL

A number base in which all numbers are expressed in groups of three bits: e.g. binary bits "10011" would be written in octal as 23.

ON LINE

Has two meanings. First and most common, means ready and available to the system, applied usually to peripherals. Second, when applied to software, means that a program or data file is on the system disks, and not on some backup medium like a tape or copy disk.

POWER SUPPLY

A computer's power supply (sometimes there is more than one) takes the AC mains voltage at one end. At the other it provides DC at the various voltages required by the computer.

RACE CONDITIONS

A race condition is when two parts of a unit unintentionally race each other to get to a certain point in that unit's operation. If a condition occurs out of sequence, having won the race, then the unit may not perform as predicted.

RAM

Short for Random Access Memory, a misnomer because ROM (see below) can also be accessed randomly. RAM, however, can be read or written into, but loses its contents when its power supply is turned off.

RECALIBRATE COMMAND

Command given to make disk heads return to the outermost point of their travel over the read/write area of a disk. Also called Return To Zero (RTZ).

REGISTER

A store place where commands (as in control register) or data may be deposited. Also a store place where data or status information may be retrieved from. All CPUs have a number of data registers, and various other types as well.

RELOCATABLE CODE

Means machine coded instructions forming a program, which can without any modification be located anywhere in memory and run successfully. (Also known as Pic-Position Independent Code).

ROM

Short for Read Only Memory; which is literally what it is: memory whose contents are written into it at manufacture, and can never be erased, even when its power supply is turned off.

SECTOR

A portion of one track. Nearly always on hard disks (as opposed to floppy disks) one sector contains 512 bytes of information.

SERVO

The electronics within a unit which control its moving parts, motors, solenoids and the like. Usually there is some feedback device attached to the moving part which feeds back into the servo electronics to aid in position assessment and stabilisation.

SOFTWARE

Programs, literature, printouts, training materials. Principally applied to programs, however.

THRASHING

Can mean two things. It can be said of a system that is swapping user jobs in and out of memory at an excessive rate, or it can mean a system being slow due to inefficient directory or file structure, when it is said to be "thrashed".

TIME SHARING

An arrangement where many users share one CPU, yet it appears to each user that they alone are using the CPU (except when too many users are using it).

UNIX

An operating system designed to be ultra-transportable between machines.
Origins at Bell telephone in the USA.

WINCHESTER TECHNOLOGY

Winchester tech disks are fixed into either their drive's cabinet – and not removable – or, more recently, sealed but removable cartridges which are only unsealed by insertion in a disk drive unit.

INDEX

A message from the publisher

Sigma Technical Press is a rapidly expanding British publisher. We work closely in conjunction with John Wiley & Sons Ltd. who provide excellent marketing and distribution facilities.

Would you like to join the winning team that published these highly successful books? Specifically, **could you successfully write a book that would be of interest to the new, mass computer market?**

Our most successful books are linked to particular computers, and we intend to pursue this policy. We see an immense market for books relating to such machines as:

DRAGON
THE BBC COMPUTER
APPLE
TANDY
SINCLAIR
OSBORNE
ATARI
IBM PC
SIRIUS
NEWBRAIN
COMMODORE
and many others

If you think you can write a book around one of these or any other popular computer — or on more general themes — we would like to hear from you.

Please write to: Graham Beech
Sigma Technical Press,
5 Alton Road,
Wilmslow,
Cheshire, SK9 5DY,
United Kingdom.

Or, telephone 0625-531035